THE
HARM
DONE

The Harm Done *is dedicated to the memory of Paul Humphrey (1958–2009).*

Paul Humphrey at tug-o'-war in Player Wills fields, St Teresa's Gardens, early 1980s
Photo: Tony O'Shea ©

THE HARM DONE

COMMUNITY AND DRUGS IN DUBLIN

Barry Cullen

First published in 2023 by SethBrimmers
Dublin
Ireland
theharmdone@gmail.com
kfcullen.ie

All rights © 2023 Barry Cullen

Paperback   ISBN: 978 1 78846 316 4
eBook   ISBN: 978 1 78846 317 1
Amazon paperback   ISBN: 978 1 78846 318 8

All rights reserved. No part of this book may be reproduced or utilised in any form or by any means electronic or mechanical, including photocopying, filming, recording, video recording, photography, or by any information storage and retrieval system, nor shall by way of trade or otherwise be lent, resold or otherwise circulated in any form of binding or cover other than that in which it is published without prior permission in writing from the publisher.

The right of the author of his work has been asserted by him in accordance with the Copyright, Designs and Patents Act 1988.

Cover design and layout by Dinky Books, Dublin
Printed in the EU

Contents

Foreword by Shane Butler		7
Introduction		11
Chapter 1	No Red Lines in Ballyfermot	19
Chapter 2	Working with Where People Are At	29
Chapter 3	Heroin in the South Inner City	43
Chapter 4	Abstinence Model for Managing Drug Problems	61
Chapter 5	A Community Fights Back	71
Chapter 6	A Doomed Youth Project, 1983–5	83
Chapter 7	Community and Political Conflict	97
Chapter 8	Community Model for Managing Drug Problems	109
Chapter 9	Not All Plain Sailing for Task Forces	123
Chapter 10	Changing the 'Unchangeable' Drug Laws	133
Chapter 11	Re-Imagining and Strengthening Community	147
Notes and References		157
Acknowledgements		175

Foreword

By his own admission, Barry Cullen had no particular interest in drug problems when, as a newly-qualified social worker, he was employed by the Eastern Health Board in the early 1980s. All this was to change when he was assigned to Dublin's south-inner city at a time when that area appeared to be awash with heroin; this so-called 'opiate epidemic' had taken both the health system and the criminal justice system by surprise, adding new difficulties to working-class neighbourhoods already struggling to cope with a wide range of socioeconomic problems. For Barry this was the start of what would turn out be an ongoing professional involvement with problem drug use, and this book is both a personal memoir and a thoughtful reflection on how Irish society has dealt with this issue over the past forty years.

Barry's assignment to a community work post in St. Teresa's Gardens, a flat complex with a high prevalence of heroin use, was on the face of it an inspired choice by the health board: a young, enthusiastic professional, whose own upbringing in Ballyfermot had convinced him of the strengths and positives to be found in urban neighbourhoods which stereotypically might be considered problem areas. However, health board commitment to the idea of collaborative working between itself and local residents proved to be tokenistic.

The health board's Community Care Programme, which had administrative responsibility for drug problems at this time, had no coherent strategy to guide its activities in relation to drug problems, and it tended to interpret the idea of community care as referring to non-institutional service provision rather than partnership with local residents' groups. Generally, health board managers subscribed to a disease model of drug addiction, which denied the causal importance of socioeconomic factors and had a naïve belief that addicts were best managed in a centralised, medically-dominated treatment service.

Not surprisingly, relationships between the health board and local community groups soured, with Barry Cullen - the board's community worker - trapped unenviably between these two factions and deciding that he had no choice except to leave the board's employment. It was not until the 1996 Rabbitte Report that governmental policy finally acknowledged the link between social deprivation and drug addiction, and through its establishment of Local Drugs Task Forces created formal structures and targeted funding schemes for locally-based responses to drug problems. To some extent, the wheel had turned full circle and Barry Cullen's last post prior to retirement was as coordinator of such a Task Force; as he sees it, these Task Forces, while 'not all plain sailing' represent progress of a kind.

Another major controversy discussed in this book concerns the most appropriate treatment outcome to be expected of addiction treatment - total abstinence or harm reduction. The first treatment services created in Dublin (the medical service at Jervis St. Hospital and the American-style therapeutic community at Coolmine) worked on the basis that, in line with international aspirations to a drug-free world and our own criminal justice sanctions against drug use, therapeutic efforts should be focused solely on getting addicts drug free and keeping them drug free. In 1989, Barry Cullen became director of the Ana Liffey Drug Project, a voluntary service based in Dublin's city centre which was the first service to openly commit itself to harm reduction, that is to assist drug users who could or not or would not remain drug free to reduce the various harms associated with their ongoing drug use. While in this position, he linked with the addiction studies programme at Trinity College so as to create public debate and policy discussion on what was obviously a thorny issue, and he would later go on to work at Trinity.

Drug addicts were not well thought of by the general public, and public policy makers were reluctant to be seen as throwing in the towel on the war on drugs or 'enabling' drug addicts to continue with their criminal ways. Over time, and largely in the context of health concerns about HIV/AIDS, harm reduction strategies such as needle and syringe exchange and methadone maintenance were introduced, and the Ana Liffey Drug Project deserves credit for its role in this process. During his time at the Ana Liffey, Barry also initiated a service user consultation process which allowed service users to express their own views on the treatment they were receiving. Service user consultation of this kind is now a standard aspiration of the country's national drug strategies, but it is far from clear that users of drug treatment services are treated with the same respect as other health service users.

The publication of this book coincides with the end stages of the country's Citizens' Assembly on Drug Use, and Barry ends his memoir with general reflections on the difficulties of reconciling health and criminal justice policy perspectives on drugs use, and with suggestions for what would generally be considered a liberalisation of current drug policy in Ireland. The tone of the book varies; there are moments of humour interspersed with puzzlement and anger, but generally the author succeeds in achieving critical distance from the complex issues discussed here. Barry Cullen has had a unique and lengthy experience as a service worker, manager and educator in this field, and his memoir is an appropriately intelligent and provocative reflection on the field into which he accidentally stumbled forty years ago.

Shane Butler
Emeritus Fellow, Trinity College Dublin

Looking down Ballyfermot Parade, early 1960s
Photo: Don Cullen

Looking down St. Teresa's Gardens, early 1980s
Photo: Derek Speirs ©

INTRODUCTION

Accidental Drug Worker

The Harm Done: Community and Drugs in Dublin, was written mainly for people who have been impacted by drug problems and those who study, work in and write about drug issues and community work and related policy. It should have a particular interest for people who, like me, entered this field from a social or youth work background.

I grew up in West Dublin during an exciting period of community activity and development that coincided with the founding of the Ballyfermot Community Association and other local bodies that advocated for community facilities and were involved with festivals, arts projects, community TV and youth services. In the mid 1970s, I was a play leader / youth worker in the local playground on Kylemore Avenue, an experience that inspired me to study at Trinity College, where I developed a special interest in social work's community influences, theories and practice. After qualifying in 1980, I worked for five years in Dublin's south inner-city, mainly in the public housing flat complex, St Teresa's Gardens.

The estate was the location of Ireland's earliest experience of clustered heroin use and in 1983 it witnessed the first forced eviction of drug dealers, during a series of anti-drugs movements. It also witnessed the first state-community partnership in response to drug problems, the ill-fated Youth Development Programme (1982–87), in which I was the second of three project leaders.

Most of my practical work since the 1980s, as well as my post-graduate studies, research and teaching, have been concerned with community and problem drug issues. My most recent employed position, 2013–21, was as coordinator of the Dún Laoghaire Rathdown Drug and Alcohol Task Force, one of twelve such bodies in Dublin city and county.

Although I have over four decades of relevant experience, I was an accidental drug worker. The drugs issue did not feature in my college lectures or practice training and, before I started to work in the south inner city, I never previously expressed interest in the topic. My main interest has been with 'community', an interest influenced by my parents' involvement in community matters, my own positive experiences of Ballyfermot's communal and street life, and my work in Ballyfermot Playground.

The concept of 'community' provides a fertile backdrop for raising and advancing social issues, including problem drug issues. It does not lend itself easily to structured political analysis, however. In academic literature, indeed, the concept of community has been described as 'slippery'[1], suggesting it is easily assigned to multiple and incongruous settings, leading to contradictory perspectives around the same issues. For example, a 'community' movement to support asylum seekers and refugees contrasts with 'community' protests against these very same groups.[2] And, amidst proposals for area regeneration, existing communities are often challenged to welcome new housing developments into their neighbourhoods and to stand down opposition to public provision.[3] Meanwhile, proposals to develop community drug services have occasionally been opposed by community groups.[4]

Historically, there have been outstanding community achievements. For example, during the era that preceded Ireland's policy of foreign direct investment, the Irish co-operatives movement helped small communities and rural villages to remain in existence, especially during large-scale emigration, rural de-population, and agricultural decline.[5] As with the credit unions,[6] the co-ops were, according to the author, Patrick Bolger, made up of ordinary people with 'unexceptional abilities' who made a significant difference in developing the communities in which they resided.[7]

In more recent times state-funded community development projects and local family resource centres[8] have played an important role in organising community members to tackle contemporary issues[9] and to develop new local services, such as child care, family support, transport, art and cultural activities.[10] As discussed in the main body of this book, community development has also played a significant role in tackling drug problems.[11] After the 2008–09 bank collapse and recession however, community development experienced significant financial cutbacks and local projects were either decommissioned or subsumed into the work of local partnership companies and most projects lost autonomy.[12]

There is a rather distinct appreciation of community in public

Introduction

housing estates, such as Ballyfermot and St Teresa's Gardens, especially if at their outset there is no given sense of place or inherited awareness of neighbourhood attachment. In many instances, the new residents experienced some disruption in their previous settlements or had to move away from familiar neighbourhoods as a result of work, changes in family circumstances or inability to afford private housing. In most instances a sense of place and identity eventually comes, usually as a result of social and economic necessity, and through community process. Although not always.

In public housing estates community development has played a role in enhancing social identity and in building both individual and collective capacities, especially when other means — financial, educational and cultural — are limited. It has also been used to represent local issues in wider policy and political domains, at times reflecting a perceived failure of established political representatives to do so. The relationship between community development and political activism, however, is fraught and, in my view, grand ideas are best left to bigger politics.

Community development, indeed, is best exercised on a small canvas where the aims and purpose are realistic and the actions focused on compact changes that are locally meaningful and tangible, particularly for grassroots members and players. The process can help community members to bring about change and improvements in their lives, and help them to appraise their own social predicaments, become more engaged in community life and involved in civil society. It can also help in mobilising people, in solidarity, around other more substantial societal problems, and issues of social justice, as these arise. However, there is a limit to what community groups can achieve within an overt political process. Too much focus on grandiose change can distort local process and dilute participation.

Community projects can make an important contribution to policy, provided the proposed policies are grounded in practice and reflect the outcomes of grassroots actions and deliberation. In this regard, community actions are best analysed, not in terms of grand narrative, but rather through the individual and collective stories told from within, leading to a tapestry of multiple theoretical-based accounts, perhaps, more than grand theory. Several insights into community are best told through everyday documented case studies and the work of local historians and heritage groups, some of whom are particularly active on social media platforms.

In broad theoretical terms, drug use is based within two contrasting,

The Harm Done

yet overlapping domains: recreational drug use whereby drugs and alcohol are consumed primarily for leisure and pleasure, and problem drug use, whereby drug consumption leads to personal, health, legal and social problems for the drug-taker and sometimes also for family members, friends, work colleagues and community members.[13]

Coming from a social work base, my primary concern is with problem drug use and more specifically demand reduction — targeted prevention, outreach counselling, medical and non-medical treatment, and rehabilitation (or recovery). For those at high-risk of losing control over their lives because of drug-use (legal and illegal), demand reduction is focused primarily on preventing or delaying the onset of serious health and social drug-related problems. For others who already have problems arising from drug use it is focused on helping them to overcome these problems. There is an array of approaches towards demand reduction, but two overall models dominate.

On the one hand there is the abstinence or disease-as-addiction model that explains drug problems in individual terms and as unrelated to socio-economic variables. It advocates that a prior commitment to abstinence is an essential prerequisite to successful treatment (see Chapter 4). On the other hand, is a community / harm reduction approach, which draws from a wider, social understanding of drug use and is focused on minimising the health and social risks. It may include abstinence as an outcome aim, but this would depend on individual circumstances (see Chapter 8). Whatever the model, treatment and rehabilitation refer to the process whereby an individual re-establishes control over their drug use such that it no longer causes them problems, even if they remain using.

When I started to work in St Teresa's Gardens and witnessed the heroin problem as it was then unfolding, my instinct was to row in with the dominant abstinence model as operated by the two main service providers, the National Drug Advisory and Treatment Centre (NDATC) and Coolmine Therapeutic Community, and to explore whether the model could be modified within a community approach. The effort was futile. Amid the general chaos then present it did not take long to realise that at its heart the disease model, for some time fixed in Government policy, was based on ideology.[14] Its main advocates viewed virtually all illegal drug-taking in terms of pathology, the disease of addiction; they viewed recovery only in terms of abstinence. They sought a single intervention for all concerned and, along the way, alternative viewpoints were castigated as dissent. Given that the model's adherents had significant influence in Government and on health authorities, initial

Introduction

efforts to develop new ideas, based on socio-economic correlates to drug problems were fraught and the proponents of change, myself included, were effectively marginalised.

In due course an alternative approach was rolled out.[15] Although framed as harm reduction, given its roots, I prefer to view this alternative as the community model, incorporating a problem drug-taking perspective. In the late-1980s and early-1990s, a range of organisations and groups argued for this alternative and helped to shape it as mainstream policy. Among its advocates with whom I had an involvement at the time — and as discussed in the chapters below — were the Ana Liffey Drug Project, Community Response, Rialto Community Drug Team and Trinity College Addiction Studies.

The community model has prevailed since the mid-1990s with drug and alcohol task forces and other local organisations and services playing a key role in providing leadership, direction and development. The model faces enormous challenges, however, not least of which is that several observers and commentators represent 'recovery' as being located primarily within medical or clinical parameters, an approach that often prevails within public and media commentary. On the community side, the model has been disproportionately affected by public expenditure cutbacks arising from the banking and financial crisis and recession 2008–14, and undermined by persistent failures to address funding restoration, and other matters.

Drawing from various work and other experiences, *The Harm Done*, written as personal narrative, provides an account of my involvement with Dublin's drug problems since their inception in the early-1980s. It is an idiosyncratic account based in the main on my personal reflections on work experiences. To keep the account short, I've omitted a lot of detail and I've refrained from drawing into the discussion several individual workers and professionals with whom I collaborated around this work. While I draw from policy and media literature, I have endeavoured to confine it to reports around relevant, recounted events, actions and policies.

It is not a full account as I refrain from any in-depth analysis of events about which I had little contemporaneous knowledge. Chronologically therefore, there are significant gaps. In particular, during 1996–2011, I worked full-time in Trinity College and although my work there encompassed relevant research, teaching and drug policy dissemination, I had little exposure to the practice field during this period.

I expect the overall account nonetheless will resonate with several commentators and observers, both those who witnessed the main events referred to and those who work in and study community and drug issues, especially within an Irish context.

In my view there is a need to completely reform drug policies, to end drugs prohibition and to legislate for new forms of regulatory control for both drugs and alcohol. Only governments can make such decisions, and common-sense political decisions in addition to deliberation — as per the 2023 Citizens' Assembly on Drugs Use — are required. Past failures, as recounted in the chapters below, contributed hugely to harm: illness, death and trauma, the destruction of community and the undermining of law. A new paradigm is needed. The same openness and creativity employed in ending the Northern Ireland Troubles (1969-98) needs to be brought to bear in bringing Ireland's 45-year-old drugs war to conclusion.

Failure to end criminal drug wars will continue to destroy, not only individuals, families and their communities, but will also undermine the fabric of society as has happened elsewhere, particularly in some illicit drug-producing countries. Alongside legislation for regulating drugs, many of those, especially young people, currently on the frontline of bringing drugs to market, need access to tangible and convincing incentives to redirect them to alternative economies and lifestyles.

Together with policy reforms, there is also a need to re-establish financial and capacity-building supports for community development. These were severely curtailed during the economic recession in 2008-14 and, shamefully, have not been restored, even though relevant national and regional development budgets have substantially increased since. In general, community policies and financial supports need a stronger focus on helping people to have a meaningful say in owning and dealing with community and drug issues, to look beyond the more visual problems of street drugs into a consideration of alcohol and the misuse of prescription drugs also towards developing appropriate, localised services.

I count myself among those who believe in the potential of community development, particularly in helping groups and communities to celebrate shared identities and to find solutions to social problems. Good leadership is central to community development and obviously access to leadership training enhances community capacities. Community is at its most successful, I believe, when it facilitates leadership development and succession whereby those seen as leaders having built their own capacities then bring to the fore people with different experiences of prevailing issues who are able, as a result, to offer fresh, alternative voices and new opportunities for development. I hope this book helps to encourage new community leaders, to motivate them to come forward and share their knowledge and insights.

In the past, community groups led out in confronting the threat from drug dealing in their communities. They established and supported harm reduction measures, and brought insight, knowledge and a problem-focused willingness to overcoming difficulties and seeking solutions. They played a critical role in transcending out-of-date approaches and ideologies. They were most effective when they looked to their own experience of drug problems to claim expertise and when they rejected attempts at professional dominance and political interference. There were setbacks but, in most instances, communities acting autonomously, were shown to have the capacities to institute and engage with new debates on drugs issues, and to confront and mitigate social exclusion. Given the opportunity and proper funding and development supports, they can continue to do so.

Ballyfermot Community Association members protesting outside City Hall, about lack of community facilities, late 1960s
Photo: Ballyfermot and St Marks Heritage Group

Kylemore Avenue Playground, Ballyfermot, 1960s
Photo: Ballyfermot and St Marks Heritage Group.

CHAPTER 1

No Red Lines in Ballyfermot

My personal interest in matters community arose from my parents — Chris (1922–2013) and Denis (1922–2002). They moved to Ballyfermot in 1952 and, at various points over the following three decades, were involved in different parish and community ventures. At its outset, Ballyfermot, with an estimated population of about 26,000 had fewer shops, pubs and facilities than many a small Irish rural town. In the Dáil chamber (parliament) local politician Seán Dunne TD (1918–69) regularly raised the issue of recreational facilities and amenities for the area. Pointing out that the estate had nearly twice the population of Waterford City, Dunne lamented its continued lack of facilities: no community centre, no place where the people had a right to meet, no public parks, no 'place where the youth can go for gymnastics and, more especially, no swimming pools to which young people can have recourse in summer time.'[1]

Enclosed by the River Liffey (north), Inchicore Railway Works (east), the Grand Canal (south) and farmland (west), all that physically lay between, initially, were houses. Later, a church, schools and shops were established followed by a dance hall, the Ritz, and Ireland's largest cinema, the Gala. Industry and warehouses eventually came also, forming a new boundary along the estate's western and southern fringes.

Our street, Ballyfermot Parade, had a hundred-and-thirty separate houses in blocks of six, all with the same grey pebble-dashed frontage, brown-stained wooden doors and window frames, white sills and grey boundary steel railings fixed to nine-inch concrete stump walls. By the late 1950s there were sixty-five streets with about eight-and-a-half-thousand units. These were small, basic and well built — two-up, two-down — with a fireplace in each room. By later standards they were overcrowded, but

The Harm Done

still had more rooms and space than residents' previous homes.

With seven children, six boys and one girl, born during 1947–62, we were an average-sized Ballyfermot family and I was the third youngest, born in 1955. On our street there were a few families of ten children or more and we were never short of players to make up the numbers in hit-the-pole soccer and other street games. For residents raised in overcrowded inner city conditions or on the periphery of rural towns, their house in Ballyfermot was their place, their castle. Outside — back and front — was their land, their domain, surrounded by an imaginary moat that enclosed their own defined space that could be shared if they chose or otherwise kept private. As the estate progressed and the street filled with cars, the house and garden boundaries became more prominent with hedges, fences, gates, driveways and several newly built porch surrounds and painted or cladded facades. These all served to mark the difference between one house and the next, between one private space and another and in how different, separate characteristics were represented

There was a lot in common — streetscapes, house colours, gardens and boundaries — but viewed from within a lot more that was different. People belonged and were assured that difference would not be rejected. They had separate roots and, as with my parents, many were uncomfortable with any expectation that they carry a single, homogenous badge of identity. In the main, community members identified as working people, but given their variable backgrounds — inner city, inner suburbs, provincial towns, and rural places — they did not all necessarily recognise or acknowledge the tag of class and were particularly uncomfortable with the labels of poor, disadvantaged and especially of deprived.

For some time residents had to put up with external attitudinal obstacles simply because their community, as a large public housing estate, was often labelled a bad area which in turn negatively affected young people's prospects of employment and social opportunities, a labelling that six decades later continues to impact on public housing.[2] My parents encouraged us to perceive labelling as a prejudice against the working class propagated by vested interests that, according to my father, resented state intrusion into housebuilding and social development and intentionally held back on public funding for basic infrastructure and facilities. He could get going on these topics when he wanted, leaving me consulting the dictionary, trying to understand his kitchen speeches, agreeing with or questioning his arguments.

Some families took labelling badly and pragmatically encouraged their children to use relatives' addresses when applying for jobs.[3] Other families simply found it difficult to adapt and survive and at the earliest opportunity transferred back to where they had come from, familiar places, extended family and other systems of established support. Most families, however, stayed and settled and, in the face of external prejudice and as an imperative to addressing their common needs, they made the estate with its streets, houses, families and children into a community.

Surrounded by a built environment, the neighbourhood today is an even larger public housing estate. More developments such as Cloverhill, Raheen and Cherry Orchard, have been added over successive decades. There were no red lines in Ballyfermot, no organised objections to additional public housing and no protests to stop Traveller dwellings. Dublin's first official Traveller settlement in Labre Park just off Kylemore Road was established with community support.[4] Although social and educational ventures were jointly developed, and some supports reciprocated, the Traveller and settled communities were mainly separate although much less so than in wealthier areas, where the red lines prevailed.

At the outset, Ballyfermot had little local commercial activity. Before the construction of the main shopping strip on Ballyfermot Road, there were only a few small shops on Grange Cross, Drumfinn, Claddagh Green and Decies Road. Near where we lived, a couple of shop vans did business on Ballyfermot Crescent and Kylemore Road. Residents regularly got the bus to Thomas Street and Meath Street to buy groceries, clothes and household items. There were few cars. When my father purchased a Morris Minor in the mid 1960s his was one of only five cars on our street. Within another decade there were so many that street play was curtailed.

Until the late 1960s there was no local industrial sector except for CIE Inchicore Works. Expansion eventually came in the shape of new manufacturing units such as the enormous Semperit tyre factory. It sat immediately south of the railway line where previously several garden allotments had thrived and where we were sometimes sent on Saturday mornings to buy fresh vegetables. The 1970s oil crisis followed by the 1980s recession resulted in many industrial units, including the tyre factory, becoming idle a little more than two decades after being built. This had a profoundly negative impact on the local population.[5] Some manufacturing was never replaced, while many buildings became used for dealerships and warehousing and other ancillary businesses.[6]

I have encountered a variety of reflections from former Ballyfermot residents on its early decades. The more nostalgic evoke memories of how ordinary people came together to settle and build a community

The Harm Done

that was at first lacking in history, facilities or a shared meaning. Others are more anxious, recalling troubled family, neighbourhood or school events. Some view it simply as a place they stayed in temporarily while they prepared for a life somewhere else.

My experience was mixed: generally happy with lots of fun and overall fulfilling. I have particularly fond memories of street play yet, at certain moments, particularly when I was required to demonstrate a physical presence, I felt estranged, frightened, more an observer than an active participant. At times I did not feel integrated, but generally there was a sense of connection that provided the foundations for eventually seeking connections elsewhere.

I am relieved that while growing up in a young family of seven children we had a stable home with secure tenure. The rent was not cheap as some would suggest, but affordable and paid once a week at the local rent office at the top of our road. My parents would have baulked at the idea of people not paying their rent and always did, and on time.

On streets and corners with friends, we only occasionally spoke to each other about our parents whom we referred to as auld wans and auld fellas. Like children everywhere, we understated their influence. Yet for me my parents had a constant presence. They had my back when needed, but they also stood up to me. At times I feared their harsh words and discipline, but mostly I relished their company and influence: my father's oft-repeated, embellished accounts of encounters with people in high places; my mother's wit, her artistic endeavours and quiet pragmatism.

They both toiled to bring in the money and maintain the household. My father always had work in the building trade, first as a carpenter and then as site foreman and clerk of works, building hotels, schools and hospital units. Family income was supplemented by his evening and weekend carpentry nixers and my mother's sewing and knitting machines. They maintained a steady, reliable hand on the tiller ensuring we were fed, clothed, kept warm and focused on doing our homework, spending time outdoors, playing on the street and going for outings, walks and hikes, moderating our differences, and reading extra books.

We were directed towards education which they viewed as key to our future prospects of work, income and family life. Apart from their expectations that we adhere to Catholic observance, they encouraged us to make up our own minds about things away from their influence. They supported us to experience other settings, to find new friends and new relationships outside their networks, be autonomous and learn and acquire independence.

No Red Lines in Ballyfermot

My parents encouraged us to speak well of Ballyfermot as they did about their childhood places: they grew up less than two kilometres apart. It was a short walk from Suir Road, Kilmainham, where my mother lived, along the Grand Canal — now Luas — and through the brewery to Pimlico in the Liberties where my father grew up. For over forty years I've lived in Rialto, equidistant from both their places. They assumed correctly that as adults we would move out of Ballyfermot, get a job, save and settle down in other places. We all live somewhere between Seattle and London, with three of the seven still in Ireland.

My parents did not experience the trauma of precarious housing and would be appalled that contemporary policies have left public housing in the doldrums. They would be particularly aghast at suggestions for reduced housing sizes, or shared units. It is not always appreciated that such plans echo, and are a legacy of, the harsh living conditions of sub-divided tenements that predominated during their youth.

Prior to Ballyfermot's establishment, there were tenement buildings in Cork Street and Allingham Street in the Liberties[7], around the corner from where my father lived before they married, and in Keogh Square, Inchicore, a short distance from where my mother was reared.[8] Some of Ballyfermot's first families originated from overcrowded tenements, which were still accommodating families during the early-1980s, when I started to work in the south inner city. Meanwhile the housing futures of those, from more recent generations, who grew up in modest public housing estates, such as Ballyfermot, now out-priced on the private market, look grim and foreboding.

Looking back, and notwithstanding its shortcomings, I feel fortunate for having been reared and formed in an urban environment. Its grey physical features, space and contours were graphically modern. By contrast, our educational and cultural exposure was traditionalist, reflecting a predominantly rural, Catholic value system, a conservative middle-Ireland polity. Meanwhile, the locus of power and leadership during Ballyfermot's first decades was within the parish, its priests and network of religious orders that managed schools and the few social services.

In the early 1960s my father was involved with a development group that included a group of residents, a local GP with his clinic at Seven Oaks, Sarsfield Road, and members of the Little Sisters of the Assumption. They tried and failed to secure parish support to develop a social centre by using an existing parish building on church grounds. In justifying his opposition to the project, parish priest Canon Michael Troy (1895–1972), according to my father, sermonised about encroaching 'O'Riordanism', a reference to the leader of the tiny Communist Party of Ireland, Michael O'Riordan (1917–2006).

My father claimed that on social issues the local church was preoccupied with hegemony more than service provision. He held socialist views, but like others involved with the proposed social centre he was far from being a communist. He was critical of Soviet and Eastern European state collectivism, believing it led directly to tyranny and the suppression of individual thought and ideas. Paradoxically, he was one of two hundred constituents who regularly voted in successive local elections for Ballyfermot's communist candidate, John Montgomery. This was because he admired Montgomery's community activism on issues such as income supports for low-paid workers and differential rents whereby the total income — including overtime and bonuses — of all working persons in a household were taken into account in assessing rents. The scheme was reformed in 1973.[9]

My father was ambivalent towards Catholicism. He was a genuine believer but yet he was constantly suspicious of the clergy. He frequently gave out yards about their quest for money and what he believed was their disdain for indigenous leaders. He was a dedicated follower, however, and somewhat intolerant of his children's occasional refusal to attend mass and confession, although his views mellowed as he grew older. My parents were committed to the church as a universal fellowship of mutual believers, and in their fifties, both were involved in church matters: she as a reader at mass and he as a communion server. They struggled greatly in reconciling their involvement with its structures. My father often entertained us in the kitchen about how he had confronted certain priests with accounts of what he had said that were highly amusing but just too unbelievable to be true.

While working in a factory near Birmingham during the Emergency he became close to a chaplain who introduced him to Catholic social teaching. He read and studied pamphlets published by the Catholic Social Guild and was influenced by the guild's writings on subsidiarity, which argued that society is best organised at lowest possible levels, and that central structures should, when possible, defer to local systems — including parish structures — in developing education, health and social policies.[10] Despite his criticisms of Church leaders — particularly Troy and the so-called 'singing priest' Michael Cleary (1934–93) whose ubiquitous presence in all matters 'community' my father found irritating — it was his faith that kept him committed, holding to the belief that the church could change from within. Like others of his generation, his Catholicism was deeply challenged by clerical scandals and abuses as revealed in the early nineties, although his faith, emboldened by decades of clerical critique, remained intact.

My mother tolerated my father's constant arguing about religion and religious leaders. Deep down she had a confident, spiritual conviction. On occasion she engaged in the politics of religion. She once confronted Cleary and told him that all she ever heard him preach was 'Michael Cleary'. However, she was more often simply interested in prayer groups and Bible readings and in trying to make sense of them in living her everyday life. Eventually she developed a stance of considering the church and its priests mostly irrelevant to her own personal beliefs and behaviours.

During the late 1960s, early 1970s, my parents were both caught up in the fervour of the Ballyfermot Community Association (BCA) and its associated local street committees and other structures. It was a microcosm of the era of civic protest: the US civil rights movements, student revolts in Paris and Berlin, the Prague Spring, and the Battle of the Bogside. People without power were questioning decision-making structures, demanding recognition and seeking status and something better for themselves and their kind.

For a while my father was a member of the BCA council. Given his argumentative character, he was inevitably involved in verbal disputes though he remained loyal to the association's aims and structures. The BCA's forerunner, a tenants' association, had differences with the parish clergy. As was typical when such disputes arose, tenants were refused access to school and church buildings for meetings and other activities. The BCA's initial demands were relatively modest, and alongside the National Association of Tenants Organisations, it sought a revision of the differential rents scheme. A national campaign in 1971 provided my first opportunity, at age fifteen, to go on a protest march around the streets of Ballyfermot.

The BCA's campaign for youth and recreational facilities, including a swimming pool, turned into a long and protracted struggle. As an interim practical response, my mother organised a swimming club. She booked regular slots in the St John of God's pool in Islandbridge and hired an instructor. Once a week she brought children from our street there, by bus, for lessons.

Through the street committee, my father organised a newsletter and held small meetings in our front parlour on community issues. He organised some outings for teenagers, including a bus trip to Enniskerry with a walk around Powerscourt House. These were successful though managing the few teenagers who were being served drink in local public houses proved challenging. In due course he found the task too much. He had ideas on policies and debates and eventually put more effort into supporting the Ballyfermot Youth Movement. It focused more on issues rather than activities.

In Ballyfermot's early decades, it was through the street committees and the leadership of the BCA and similar bodies that community members gained the confidence to do things for themselves, to assert their own leadership rather than relying on parish and other structures. Some priests, including John Wall (1942–2020) and Peter Lemass (1933–88) brought a modern perspective and were open to having a background role with local ventures, such as the Peace Corps and a Latin American parish support group. Others, including Troy and some of his successors, were more used to dominating community matters and used the power of the pulpit to suppress emerging grassroots initiatives. In the early 1950s, for example the Inchicore and Ballyfermot co-operative was castigated by Troy and forced to close.[11]

During its initial stages the BCA, which prioritised the need for its own community centre, was distinctly non-clerical if not anti-clerical. It is instructive that its street committee structure had its genesis in street soccer leagues. Playing soccer was forbidden on church and school lands and Troy and other priests were disdainful of that 'foreign game'. At one stage, Troy succeeded in getting local authority officials to dig up the flat section of the California Hills, an open field opposite his home on Le Fanu Road, thereby preventing the children from playing soccer. In its early days the BCA constituted a formidable challenge to the church's monopoly on community leadership.

Contemporary Ballyfermot's tradition and social identity starts not with stories from the original rural townland, but with tales its families brought at their point of settlement. Memories of place are important. For the first generation, including myself, it starts with our accounts of an estate just getting off the ground at the point of our birth, how sparse physical settings influenced our decisions, informed us in our choices and their parameters, and constructed for us the spaces within which we played, exchanged and developed relationships.

Through the BCA, the Peace Corps, Ballyfermot Youth Movement, Ballyfermot Community TV, sports bodies and local youth clubs, St Mary's and OLV (Our Lady of Victories), the estate's first generations were assisted in preparing for societal roles, leadership and employment. Today, arising from the pioneering work of these bodies and founders several community projects dealing with education, childcare, family support, drug problems, the arts, and community employment flourish. They simply would not be there without the hard work undertaken by Ballyfermot's first residents, the pioneers who settled into an estate that had little but housing. Through dedication and determination, they asserted an indigenous leadership and made Ballyfermot, originally devoid of facilities and services and dominated by Catholic conservatism, into a vibrant community, albeit one that continues to struggle.

Patricia Kelleher, Mary Whelan and Olivia O'Leary at the launch of Dublin Communities in Action, 1992.
Photo: Barry Cullen

A youth employment action group protesting with the support of former IRA Chief of Staff, Government Minister, and winner of both the Nobel and Lenin international peace prizes, Sean McBride (1904–1988), in early 1980s
Photo: Derek Speirs ©

CHAPTER 2

Working with Where People Are At

As a teenager, I occasionally attended an evening youth club in the playground — the Layer — at the top of our road, and in 1975, two years after leaving school, I signed up for a part-time youth-work training course. Through this I got to know the playground leader Elizabeth Durham (1925–2001) who had been appointed to her senior position a few years previously. When I was a child, playground staff were referred to as Brother or Sister even though they were unaffiliated to religious orders. Durham was initially known to me as Sister Durham, but then discarded the moniker for Mrs Durham.

While attending the course, Durham asked if I would be interested in applying for a vacant position in the playground. I had recently dropped out of studying engineering in Trinity College and was at a loose end, looking for work and considering a few administrative job offers in the civil service and with a construction company. My interest in the youth-work course was more as a volunteer, but I was attracted to the prospect of working in the playground as I admired Durham who had struggled greatly to raise a family of five after her husband's untimely death. Outwardly she came across as austere, but this belied her deep affinity for people who struggled in life. I could see she had a modern vision for the playground not simply as a place where children randomly played, but as a focal point that could help make a significant difference in the lives of the children — and their parents.

She had established a pre-school service a few years earlier. During the 1970s, the labour market was overwhelmingly male and, in general, public policy supported the constitutional assertion that society was best served when mothers remained within the family home rather than engaging in outside employment. The marriage bar required women to retire from public sector employment when they married. Differential pay scales for men and women — in public and private sectors — was only abandoned following Ireland's accession in 1973 to the European Union, then known as the European Common Market. It introduced work equality measures.

Durham had Catholic convictions, but she also had feminist leanings. In setting up the pre-school she wanted to provide places to the children of local mothers returning to work. She was acutely aware that several mothers bringing their children to the pre-school were under stress with money, difficult marital relationships and, in some cases, domestic violence. She felt compelled to help in relieving these difficulties.

On a personal level, she was mindful of her own need to get out and work having become widowed more than a decade earlier. Doing so had helped her to adopt a broader, more liberal, confident perspective. The pre-school was an arena in which she could engage with parents. She built relationships and heard the problems and issues that dominated their lives. She helped in framing a response to presenting difficulties. Inevitably, this work led her to organise information, advice and workshops on health and related matters, including contraception and domestic violence. She helped women get access to vital health and legal services when needed.

Her approach was considered radical at the time. The playground was managed through the Catholic Youth Council, a sub-committee of the diocese's Catholic Social Service Conference, now known as Crosscare, which ran the food centre in Ballyfermot. Her employers lacked the commitment to provide child care and women's health advice and were averse to contraceptive information. Mrs Durham had the support of her immediate manager however, Louis O'Neill who was Head of Playgrounds. He also brought innovation to the work with young people, and established successful youth holiday centres in Oakwood, Co. Wicklow and Coolure House, Co. Westmeath.

In addition to the Catholic church, the state also was disinterested in child care. It was described by the leading pre-school body at the time as resistant to 'breaking the ties between mother and child on any account'.[1] The state also, having failed in a constitutional challenge on its decision to seize contraceptive devices at the point of importation[2], subsequently colluded in suppressing information on the topic. The Censorship of Publications Board in 1976 banned a booklet, *Family Planning,* by the Irish Family Planning Association that promoted sales of condoms. This ban was lifted a year later following a successful High Court challenge.[3] Durham was not alone in her endeavours around child care as various bodies involved in community development elsewhere, particularly Ballymun, Crumlin, the north and south inner city, viewed community playgroups and women's health issues as critical components of community engagement.

The playground had a daily routine and structure. Managing the use and sharing of equipment, swings, tennis bats, balls, footballs and board games was obviously key to the work. We staff moved through the playground space, mediating disputes and being available to protect those finding it hard to get a turn on the equipment. We watched over free play and when it was evident the children were running out of ideas, we organised team games. All the while we sought out opportunities to engage more directly in their learning and development. We often sat with them individually or in small groups. In even the most difficult home circumstances they showed incredible positivity about their families. It was clear that some carried a lot of additional adult home responsibilities. Through slowly building relationships with those who were troubled we were able to support them discreetly in mitigating the impact of difficult personal and family matters.

In addition to playground work I was asked to develop and oversee evening clubs and similar activities for young people. The most important of these was one I ran for young men and women aged eighteen plus who were considered on the edge, found themselves outside of employment and who were highly involved in drink and drugs. Some were involved in petty criminality. The club met once a week on Thursday evenings and became known as the Thursday Club. It was a safe haven, a place where the group could assemble, play cards, pool, darts and engage in conversation, without drink or drugs.

Two separate types of person then known to me were using drugs. On one side were members of the Thursday Club and similar, who shared stolen prescription tablets, usually barbiturates, that they mixed with cheap cider and cough bottles. These they bought from a pharmacy near the Werburgh Street dole office that stocked up with Phensedyl syrup on sign-on and collection days. They occasionally used cannabis, but in general this drug was not affordable and thus purchased only when they had extra money.

On the other side were a few groups — referred to collectively as heads — who regularly used cannabis recreationally in much the same way that others used alcohol although some tended to drink also. A few pubs in the city centre were known to turn a blind eye to cannabis smokers as long as it was discreet. A nightclub, Osibisa, was a place where drug-

The Harm Done

taking was pervasive. Whether drink or cannabis, this group could afford their intake through work or other income. The cannabis was usually sourced through friendship networks and the alcohol obviously was legally purchased.

For a while, and after a lot of preparation, Thursday Club members got involved in organising activities, including discos, for younger teenagers. These proved successful and I have met people since who continue to cherish their memory. It was particularly successful for club members. Whereas the adult community perceived them as street drinkers, drug and cough bottle users and potential troublemakers, the fact that they could, albeit under supervision, successfully operate youth activities and discos gave them currency. It improved their local reputation and standing and helped some of them to develop and reinforce pathways to stability.

The following year in summer 1976, while Durham was on sabbatical leave I was appointed the playground's acting leader-in-charge with additional responsibility for developing a summer project. In addition to temporary summer playground staff it was decided to buy in specialised groups in drama, arts and music — including the Children's T-Company — and to involve parents and other community members in organising and developing the activities.

The T-Company were an impoverished yet highly creative group. Individual members later had successful careers in theatre, cinema, poetry, comedy and literature. In the playground they improvised workshops with various groups including the Thursday Club, from which they developed a show entitled One Bad Apple. This was a raw mix of songs, colourful visuals and set-piece drama, telling the story of a young man involved in crime desperately struggling to avoid becoming a bad apple.

Other shows were similarly engaging, funny, full of colour with lots of music and songs. They did a magical mystery tour that involved taking fifty children on a bus journey. During the trip, they 'coincidentally' witnessed a staged kidnapping where the victim — a member of the T-Company and known to them through previous activities — was bundled into a car and driven away. The tour continued with the bus giving chase to the kidnappers' car until the children eventually captured them at the Hell Fire Club in the Dublin Mountains. It was a remarkably successful, magical event. Many of the children and adults had never experienced anything quite like it before.

Summer 1976 was the warmest on record. The sunny weather contributed to a unique playground atmosphere. With regular outdoor

Working with Where People Are At

T-Company shows and art and drama workshops, at times it felt akin to the opening carefree dance scene from the 1961 film West Side Story. I revelled in my first opportunity to lead a project, in being able to organise things with new ideas, especially across arts, drama and other creative activities.

During my eighteen months with the playground, I had weekly call-in discussions and meetings at the Catholic Youth Council (CYC) office. It administered the playgrounds and was located in a former parochial building on Arran Quay. CYC's director was a priest and some administrative staff were nuns. There was a sense that other staff were either close to or had themselves once been clerics. There were regular opportunities for open debate among staff from the different community playgrounds, especially during these call-in days and the occasional seminar or workshop. These tended to be practical, how-to events, on committee structures, producing leaflets, newsletters, publicity, and so on. There was also debate around wider issues, however.

The work of the European Commission's First Programme on Pilot Schemes and Studies to Combat Poverty (1974–80)[4] had commenced. Within some communities and organisations involved in the programme debate on community participation, work and development was robust. Often an important distinction was made between projects that were established to provide social services to local people and other projects that saw the same people in central, organisational and leadership roles. That this debate was going on at all had an impact on the discussions among field staff in the CYC and elsewhere.

Once, I visited staff in the playground in Sheriff Street and they told me about work being undertaken by local people involved with the North Centre City Community Development Association (NCCCDA). This had a community project funded through the European Commission's poverty programme. Some members were developing a TV documentary with the working title, It's a Hard Auld Station.[5] Broadcast by RTÉ later in the year and narrated by local residents Tessie McMahon, Johnny Murdiff and Mick Rafferty, it was a raw, grounded analysis of the impact of a declining economy on the area's social structure. It was my first exposure to an alternative documentary analysis of urban poverty through popular media. Previously, in 1971, RTÉ's current affairs flagship programme Seven Days ran a controversial TV report that brought attention to the absence of social facilities for disaffected youth in Ballyfermot.[6]

While the Seven Days report was brave and a genuine attempt to raise and discuss social issues in the public domain, it drew considerable

The Harm Done

criticism for what were seen as exaggerated — and allegedly staged — images of young people congregating together in a local field to drink cider. It was perceived as an unfair and demeaning outsider representation of Ballyfermot, undertaken without adequate insider involvement. Some criticisms, particularly that the programme lacked local engagement, were valid. Others, especially those articulated by political and church leaders, sought to undermine legitimate emerging concerns similar to those represented by local people in the north inner city. The work on It's a Hard Auld Station was a radical departure to get this type of direct representation of working peoples lived experiences.

The focus on people's participation was being developed in other European funded projects in Dublin's south inner city, Connemara, Cork, Donegal and Waterford. Through this work people were encouraged to develop their own narratives, lending their voices to the need for change and development and for identifying and accessing resources and underused properties and facilities. During my later studies at Trinity College I undertook practice visits to the projects in Donegal and Dublin's south inner city, and we had a class visit to the project in Letterfrack, Connemara.

The South City Project, based in Meath Street in Dublin's Liberties, had a focus on welfare information and researching health and education needs.[7] It supported local people to produce a newspaper, *Liberty People* which reported that community workers in the south inner city had been trying, with little success, to bring about a united association of community bodies throughout the area. An organisational and representational difficulty arose as a result of a public campaign, during the late 1970s, against the siting of Dublin Corporation offices at the Viking site at Wood Quay (in 2002 Dublin Corporation became Dublin City Council). Campaign activists occupied the site and claimed they had the support of the 'people of the Liberties'. Residents claimed, however, that none of the twelve autonomous local tenant bodies had been consulted and the activists' proposals for alternative developments, including a hotel and museum, lacked local relevance. It appeared that the tag Liberties had been expropriated for use by an external body that had archaeological objections to local authority plans. By not having a united local voice, the interests of local community organisations remained silent.[8]

In Donegal political tension arose as a result of the project organising home-knitters to develop their own co-operative for sourcing wool, sales and marketing. Existing middlemen contacted politicians to have the project stopped, unsuccessfully as it turned out. These representations exacerbated tensions between the national committee managing the projects and the then government minister responsible, future taoiseach Charles Haughey (1925–2006). He was disdainful of what he once described as a 'tuppence halfpenny committee' and its work.[9]

Between these and other developments, people's participation was to become a key element in future community programmes and interventions, nationally and locally. It was particularly evident in the work of the Combat Poverty Agency (1986–2009), the Community Development Programme (1990–2010), Local Drug and Alcohol Task Forces (1997–), the Pilot Community Development Programme (2021–) and other locally based initiatives.

Arising from my work in the playground, I went to Trinity College in October 1976 as a student in economic and social studies. While I had gained useful practical and group-work experience, I wanted to refine and develop this. I was hungry for social sciences knowledge and the faculty included degree courses in business, economics, sociology, social work and politics. The period 1976–80 was an exciting time to study social sciences. It coincided with the winding down of children's residential institutions and reformatories, a strengthening of the women's movement, and the growing impact of protest groups in the US, Europe and elsewhere.

Irish social work was seriously underdeveloped. Religious bodies were the main providers of services that fitted a social work description and they thereby continued, if not reinforced, a religious charity tradition established in the 19th century across a range of other domains. These included nursing, hospital care, teaching, children's residential care and the care of those in need in community settings.[10] Under the careful watch of Archbishop John Charles McQuaid (1895-1973), the post-Emergency expansion of Ireland's welfare services diverged from the UK and European welfare state norm and offered a distinctly Catholic, parish-based ethos in tandem with religious-run residential services.

By the late 1960s, the model began to unwind in the face of emerging social issues and declining numbers of new entrants into religious life. The aims of keeping the state out of the home and away from dealing with child and family issues was no longer sustainable. In crafting a new health system for a modernising society, a social dimension was inevitable. Following the 1970 Health Act that set up regional health boards, the state for the first time began to employ trained, qualified social workers in significant numbers: from three in the Eastern Health Board area in 1974 to fifty, two years later.[11] In due course many of these worked on the frontline in community, child welfare and family services.

The Harm Done

On occasion, particularly where no local health structures previously existed, newly-recruited social workers were assigned to work closely with religious personnel in parish centres. This practice ended within a few years, chiefly as social workers became concerned at not receiving adequate support, guidance and supervision. In addition, their office facilities were frequently adorned with religious icons and some felt misused as quasi-pastoral workers.

Remnants of the pastoral approach were still in place after I qualified and started working for the health board. For instance, three of the seven members of the social work team I joined in 1980 were members of religious orders, of whom two were funded on a block-grant basis to provide social work services. The senior social worker running the team was also a nun.

Individual religious social workers incorporated a Catholic social care ethos into their work. Some coupled this with an established secretive practice in their response to issues such as pregnancy outside of marriage and domestic violence. Others were more progressive. In general there was an over reliance on hidden-away religious-owned institutions for providing solutions to everyday social problems and it was taken for granted that the care they offered was appropriate, safe and secure.

Unmarried pregnant women were regularly encouraged, often pressurised, to have their babies in religious-run institutions where their children were then placed for adoption. Meanwhile, parish-based responses to domestic violence frequently prioritised the preservation of marriage and occasionally children were placed temporarily in nearby children's residential homes. Their parents were given respite and individually encouraged to resolve their 'differences'. Inevitably, such short-term placements transformed into either long or erratic periods of placement, corresponding to erratic yet persistent episodes of continued marital violence.

While the Catholic church and religious bodies have been rightly criticised for these practices, it was obvious, especially to growing numbers of social workers and other frontline personnel, that this approach had been fashioned over the decades through state support and encouragement. During the 1970s a regular topic of discussion at formal health board meetings was 'unwanted' pregnancies, a term reflecting the official social service mindset of the time.

These practices were institutionalised. It would take decades to dismantle them, especially, as in the case of care homes and other residential services, there were few state-operated alternatives, and as observed by author Tony Fahey, there was no reserve funds 'within the public system which could easily have been drawn upon to fill gaps caused by withdrawal or non-activity on the part of the church'.[12] In general social workers brought a new perspective, particularly in relation to pregnant young women. Although many continued to reside in care homes while awaiting the birth of their children they were visited by social workers who explored with them a range of suitable options other than those presented by the religious managers. They also provided advice on welfare entitlements and other supports that could be available in the event they held on to their babies.

In the absence of state provision it was to religious bodies such as the Daughters of Charity that a new wave of health board child care managers turned to establish alternative non-residential child welfare services.[13] Also the decline in the number of religious vocations correlated with an increasing tendency by some individual religious to re-define their mission and to engage in activities that were represented as opting for the poor. During the 1970s, Threshold — which provides information and advice to private tenants and also advocates for legislative reform — was founded by a Capuchin priest, while the Jesuit priest, Peter McVerry began outreach work with young homeless in the north inner city, eventually leading to him founding the Arrupe Society (later renamed the Peter McVerry Trust).[14]

During the 1970s, service user groups, the women's movement, and internal figures within Church bodies, challenged established secretive, practices. They advocated as an alternative the need for safety, shelter and specific designated services, particularly for women and young people who were homeless. In college seminars and workshops, we were encouraged to incorporate secular perspectives. In our classroom seminars, issues of domestic violence, contraception and child care provision came to the fore. There were several workshops and talks organised by student societies with speakers from newly-established secular bodies such as Women's Aid (domestic violence), Cherish (lone parents), HOPE (youth homeless) and the Well Woman Centre (family planning). Talks on emerging voices within the church were organised also. The college St Vincent de Paul society organised for Peter McVerry to give a talk about his work with young homeless in the north inner city.

In Trinity College I built up a good relationship with my tutor Noreen Kearney (1934–2019), and later worked with her when she chaired the Combat Poverty Agency. Kearney was an accomplished networker and highly respected in teaching and practice roles. She stood out in her ability to occupy internal leadership functions as head of school and dean of the faculty, as well as equally important and challenging external leadership roles in the statutory and non-governmental sectors. These included the Eastern Health Board, Charter Board Rotunda Hospital, Combat Poverty Agency and Katharine Howard Foundation.

In my final year, I had an excellent course on community work given by Mary Whelan (1941–2022) who in later years was the interim director of the Combat Poverty Agency (1985–87), and founded the national organisation CAN (Community Action Network). To this day CAN provides leadership development, human rights work, and offers other supports to community organisations. Whelan was highly influenced by the writings of Paulo Freire (1921–97).[15] She was a purveyor of hope in community work and a believer in making big things possible through small beginnings. She frequently used the phrase 'start where people are at', to ensure we were grounded in our practice.

Along with Patricia Kelleher, Whelan wrote *Dublin Communities in Action* (1992). It provides a detailed account of the origins, practices, progress and issues arising in community development projects in Blanchardstown, Fatima Mansions, the north inner city, and Tallaght and has a brief historical overview of community development in Ireland.[16] Through her teaching I had access to good written material and ideas on community social work and intervention models[17] and the potential role social workers could play in viewing their transactional role as relating not only to the individuals with whom they work but to their environments, and surrounding systems, also.[18] In Whelan's view, community work's role was to try to change the institutions and systems that contributed to and reinforced people's poverty and exclusion. She was wary of casework's limitations. She rejected the idea that the purpose of the worker's relationship with people was in modifying their social behaviours and adaptation to the societal mainstream. For Whelan the worker also had to engage with wider issues.

The community approach was outlined at the time by UK author Marjorie Mayo in her reflections on the 1960s US War on Poverty programme and the UK's Community Development Programme operating in the early 1970s. Inevitably within these a structural analysis of poverty's causes as distinct from one based on individual deficits or motivations, emerged.[19] Given the tensions arising from these contrasting perspectives — similar to those that arose later in the Irish Programme[20] — neither programme survived beyond the pilot phase.

Mayo warned that community development could as easily be used to co-opt and repress groups as to empower them. She noted, however, that while community did not necessarily create a movement for significant social change, it did potentially contribute to local struggles around immediate tangible needs. Mayo's analysis had echoes of Mary Whelan's position and her emphasis on working with people, where they were at, in order to bring about small but discernible changes.

My practical community work placement was with Mick Casey[21]. He undertook his Masters in Toronto, Canada, in community development, urban renewal and alternatives in education. He had community experience in inner city Detroit and New York, in addition to the Dublin suburbs of Artane, Coolock and Killester. He was familiar with and supported liberation theology, a Latin American movement that extended the message of Vatican II towards the formation of grassroots organisations dedicated to restoring social justice in human relations.

Like Whelan, Casey was highly influenced by the writings of Paulo Freire, who argued that many formal models of community education and engagement had limited positive impact on poor people and offered little opportunity for them to transform their social position. Freire, whose background was in education, advocated that community workers needed a participative model, thereby assisting people to develop a better understanding of their position in society and to assert self-learning and leadership in bringing about change through bottom-up, grassroots organisations.[22]

Casey drew guidance from Vatican II and the principle of the whole parish — laity, religious and clergy alike — participating together in critical issues affecting community life. He was involved in developing a community project around Sean McDermott Street that emphasised education, employment and training services for young people. After a few years using small grants to organise a youth unemployment action group and to undertake youth outreach and drop-in, a crafts centre and community services, the project, with significant funds from the newly-established Youth Employment Agency, evolved into Lourdes Youth and Community Services.[23] It was formally established in 1984 and continues today with an even wider range of local services and programmes. The project also moved from being based within the parish to coming under the management of a local group.

The north inner city was considered one of the most socially disadvantaged areas in the country: almost two-thousand family units continued to live in Victorian tenement buildings on Sean McDermott Street, Gardiner Street and in Summerhill. Most buildings were overcrowded and barely habitable, contributing to problems of health, stress and poor quality of life. The area was badly affected by the containerisation of the docks area, which almost single-handedly killed off traditional routes to unskilled local employment.

As part of this placement I utilised the college's audio-visual facilities to compile a video documentary, Tomorrow's Playground, that dealt with development issues. At the time it was planned to build a motorway — the Eastern Bypass — through the community, demolish the tenements and depopulate the area. The remainder of my time was spent shadowing other local workers, including social worker Fergus McCabe (1949–2020), leader of a community project working with young people deemed at social and educational risk.

The project was established following publication of the *Interim Report of the Task Force on Child Care Services* (1975) that recommended setting up pilot neighbourhood youth projects. One was started in the north inner city with McCabe as project leader. A second was intended for a north Dublin suburb, but following initial difficulties it was moved to Fatima Mansions, Rialto (see Chapter 3). Through linking with work colleagues and local community activists, McCabe helped to create a united local structure, the previously mentioned North Centre City Community Development Association (NCCCDA). This aimed to support self-advocacy on behalf of local people and drew inspiration from the tenants movement NATO and the Dublin Housing Action Committee.[24]

The NCCCDA mobilised the community against planning proposals to depopulate the area. That mobilisation led to a successful campaign in 1979 to elect their own independent community candidate Tony Gregory (1947–2009) to Dublin City Council. Before the election, council officials reportedly refused to meet NCCCDA representatives saying they dealt only with councillors on planning matters. Gregory's election changed all that. In 1982, he was elected as an independent community TD and for nine months held the balance of power in supporting a minority government led by Charles Haughey. For a short time, he succeeded in reversing policy for the area through new house-building, a new school and putting into place financial supports for various community projects.

As with the Ballyfermot Community Association, the NCCCDA became the foundation for several community-based projects and services many of which continue to operate successfully in the area four decades on. Looking back, it is almost unreal to reflect that community approaches in Ballyfermot, the north inner city and elsewhere were at the time considered radical. Clearly they were a pragmatic community response

Working with Where People Are At

to people being denied opportunities to participate in determining their own needs and services in a highly centralised administrative and political system. They were viewed as radical perhaps because previously there was little political or administrative interest in these issues. And it is remarkable that it was not until poorer urban communities began to assert leadership and control over their own affairs that they became noticed.

Young people with Terrie Kearney in the Small Club, St. Teresa's Gardens, late 1970s.
Photo: Courtesy Terrie Kearney

A block of flats, that had become associated with large-scale drug dealing, is demolished in Fatima Mansions in the late 1980s
Photo: Clodagh Boyd ©

CHAPTER 3

Heroin in the South Inner City

After qualifying from Trinity College in October 1980 I started work as a community social worker with the Eastern Health Board (EHB). This was one of eight regional health authorities that three decades later were replaced by a single body, the Health Services Executive (HSE). The EHB included counties Dublin, Kildare and Wicklow. These were sub-divided into ten sub-regional areas. I was based in Community Care Area 3[1], that stretched from Dublin's southwest inner city to Harold's Cross, Terenure, Rathfarnam and beyond. The population exceeded 100,000. Most referrals into the community team of seven social workers were from a few inner city estates (flats): Bridgefoot Street, Dolphin House, Fatima Mansions and St Teresa's Gardens, all built in the 1950s and 1960s, along with Oliver Bond House and Marrowbone Lane, built during the 1930s. Between them these estates — all in Dublin 8 postal district — accounted for less than 8,000 people, but they easily made up about 90% of social work referrals, whether through expressed need or prevailing priorities.

On my first day, the social worker I was replacing drove me around the whole catchment area and brought me to a social services centre in the southwest inner city. I was introduced to a member of the social work team, Irene Bailey. She belonged to the Little Sisters of the Assumption and originally she was assigned to the area as caseworker by her congregation. She was concerned that casework had limited impact in the midst of the area's needs. After undertaking social work training, she applied for a health board position as community worker.[2] The recruitment of community workers, or assignment of social workers to community work roles, resulted from a 1977 Department of Health memorandum through which thirty 'community work' posts were created nationally, reflecting a

The Harm Done

'willingness by the Health Boards ... to recognise that the time has now come to concentrate on community as a means of prevention and for the provision of the most relevant and flexible services'.[3]

The memorandum specified that the community workers would have a role in identifying social needs, generating an awareness of these needs, advising on priorities, promoting and supporting local voluntary groups and linking with other statutory bodies in developing local responses. It was considered a progressive measure at the time, especially as the memorandum stated that community development should 'lead to a consciousness of living in a fairly well-defined community, with shared interests and shared responsibilities, making the community aware of its opportunities and, as far as is possible, meet these needs, be based on values and use approaches which respect the innate capacity of each individual and do not necessarily create dependence'. It was clear that Bailey was more enthused about this role.

I also met Alan Hendrick who was developing a Neighbourhood Youth Project (NYP) for Dolphin House and Fatima Mansions and community playgroup coordinator Mary Doheny who supported several pre-school services throughout the south inner city, including Fatima Mansions, Oliver Bond House and St Teresa's Gardens. As Hendrick worked on his own, without staff, I was assigned a role of supporting him in his role.

In the social services centre all three spoke about difficult local issues and the various efforts that were being made to resolve them. Low-key pre-school playgroups, summer projects and family supports were considered the bedrock of community activity, particularly in terms of generating people's participation, as well as providing services to children and young people. Community members also worked alongside Dublin Corporation to regularise tenancies of some people who were squatting, although it was believed that a small number was using the flats for criminal activities.

In less than twelve months after starting my job as a social worker, I was assigned to a community work role alongside Bailey. It was a dream appointment. Since working in the Ballyfermot playground I had cherished a community work position and after graduating I was enthused about the role within a social work framework. My predecessors — Terrie (Therese) Kearney and Patricia Daly — had been active in the previous six years in supporting small-scale community projects in line with the above mentioned Department of Health memorandum. They helped people with leadership and volunteer training, to access financial and other resources, and to operate various local activities. Inevitably, they focused on developing a response to the drug problem, which clearly constituted an identification of new social needs.

I linked up with the St Teresa's Gardens Development Committee in their premises, the Small Club, a former ground-floor shop consisting of four small (twelve sq m) rooms on Donore Avenue at the estate's entrance. The building was rundown, and the windows were blocked up. There was little light, and it badly needed renovation. Committee members sat on rickety chairs around an old metal table, flanked by two electric heaters while a mild draught blew in through badly fitted metal doors. The centre was typical of other under-funded facilities set aside for community use at the time. In addition to small community meetings it was also used for a playgroup, youth and after-school activities. There was no designated manager or cleaner and all the maintenance and other work was undertaken voluntarily by committee members and other volunteers.

In contrast to their modest facilities, committee members Matt Bowden, Thomas Conlon, Paul Humphrey (1958–2009), Willie Martin, John Moylan, May O'Connell, Harriet Reddy and Margaret Williams were all young and enthusiastic residents with a deep affection for their community and for exploring practical ways to improve it. Their conversations began with reflections on recent youth events, such as the local disco and youth outings, as well as concerns that certain young people were being led astray and whether there was a need to speak to their parents. Other discussions centred on Corporation officials and complaints about the maintenance of flats and communal areas. Relations with local authority staff were particularly strained arising from a dispute in 1979 during which residents dumped their rubbish onto Donore Avenue, at the entrance to the flats. A fracas followed and the gardaí became involved.[4]

Despite community adversities, the group had an air of optimism, confidently working at getting things done and seeking improvements. They had a lot of support from a newly appointed priest, Sean McArdle, who helped them access parish premises for youth activities and other resources. As a trained electrician, he helped in practical ways by fixing the electrical wiring in community facilities and sometimes in people's homes.

Committee members were particularly concerned about the drug problem. They had first detected it two years previously during an outreach club operated by Terrie Kearney and local volunteers. Both Kearney and committee members had remarkably similar recollections of the period. Youths were coming to the club intoxicated and they were surprised to realise the young people's changing moods were provoked by drugs as opposed to alcohol, their usual expectation. Research on detached youth at the time showed no evidence of drug-taking, but lots of reports on alcohol misuse, criminality and rough sleeping.[5] The volunteers became worried when the youths excluded them from secret discussions. This worry quickly turned to alarm when they realised the main drug of use was heroin and by then most of those involved were injecting. Local leaders had been led to believe that only young people who had previously used the so-called gateway drug cannabis would move on to heroin. They were understandably shocked at the emergence of this new drug use.

Previously Ireland's drug scene was based around the activities of established small-time dealers who (see Chapter 2) imported relatively small amounts of cannabis to share with trusted friends. The Government's successful clampdown on armed bank robberies during the late 1970s — a move motivated by concern that the IRA was using such activity to raise funds for its armed struggle — meant that gangs previously involved in these activities turned their attention to drug importation. It was an alternative funding source, a development that put small-time drug importers and dealers out of business.[6]

With organised criminals now involved, inner city neighbourhoods became a prime location for drug dealing. They were especially attractive to the family gang that included Larry Dunne (1948–2020)[7], originally from the south city suburb of Crumlin — 15 minutes walking distance from St Teresa's Gardens. Dunne had a reputation for armed robbery. It is often claimed that he was singularly responsible for bringing heroin to Ireland, a claim that is as facetious as the one that banker Sean Fitzpatrick (1948–2021) alone introduced reckless lending practices during the 1990s and 2000s. The conditions for both developments were already present and were linked to global events. In banking, an expansion in cheap money supply internationally led to risky property-related lending. As for heroin, changes in global supply routes in Afghanistan, Iran and Pakistan arising from war, revolution and other conflicts demanded new markets. If Dunne had not brought in heroin, someone else would.

Indeed in the late 1970s–early 1980s, the influx of drugs into Ireland was experienced in several UK and other European cities. As in Dublin, heroin use previously was low-key, sporadic and associated with occasional middle-class use, including healthcare professionals with easy access to medicinal supplies.[8] During the 1970s relatively small numbers presented for drug treatment, usually resulting from use of cannabis, hallucinogens, amphetamines and barbiturates. Little use of opiates was reported.[9] Drug services were framed within the overall structure of individually-oriented psychiatric interventions.[10] Unlike other psychiatric disorders for which there was a national network of mental health facilities, though, drug problems were treated within a single specialist treatment centre, the National Drug Advisory and Treatment Centre (NDATC). This was formed in the late 1960s in Jervis Street Hospital, Dublin.

At a policy level the problem generated little other than occasional concern.[11] Previously in the late 1960s when the drug problem as a whole was relatively minor, Government set up a working party to consider developments. In 1971 this reported there was no concern about 'the illicit supply of heroin', but that the 'position should not be viewed with complacency lest such supplies become available.'[12] In recognising the potential threat arising from drug use the Oireachtas passed the Misuse of Drugs Act 1977.[13] It updated Irish law and distinguished between having drugs for personal use and having them for sale or supply. Penalties for cannabis were more lenient than for possession of other drugs.

From the late 1970s, attendees at the NDATC increased from 294 in 1979 to 1,314 in 1983, due mainly to heroin. Unlike previous facility users these new clients were, in the main, from traditional public housing estates, in particular communities that, after the closure of mainstay low-skill industries during the 1970s, were affected by high levels of redundancy, unemployment, poverty, educational under-achievement and environmental decline.

As in Dublin, researchers identified and tracked these same developments in UK cities such as Edinburgh, Glasgow, Liverpool and London.[14] In turn, the problems arising from heroin were found to have contributed to other social and environmental problems, especially at local level.[15] Several actors in the criminal field were willing and able to become involved in Dublin's new drug business. Some had more visibility and therefore more notoriety. They had easy access to flats complexes and established business within these locations without great effort. Their nefarious activities had huge negative impact on their young victims. Moreover, drug dealers' innocent family members and friends inevitably paid a heavy price, particularly as a result of media and public attention that accrued from their appalling behaviours.

Following an upsurge in hepatitis B presentations in the south inner city, local GP Fergus O'Kelly, having detected a group of patients who developed infections as a result of injecting heroin in 1979, made a notification to the public health authorities. Similarly, at around

The Harm Done

the same time, Terrie Kearney informed health board officials of the growing problem. In a report in March 1980, she urged them to 'adopt the tactics of targeted information, outreach counselling and the training of local concerned persons'. O'Kelly corroborated Kearney's information especially when she requested the then Health Education Bureau (HEB) to put in place a customised, targeted preventative programme for young people. The HEB, set up as a semi-state body in the mid-1970s, was unwilling to create such targeted programmes that acknowledged the effect of socioeconomic deprivation on the prevalence of drug problems. Instead, it favoured universalist prevention schemes that focused on individual decision-making, across all socio-economic populations.

Kearney was taken aback by the discouraging responses to her proposals. It suggested nobody with any real authority accepted her account that a major unprecedented epidemic of heroin-use was unfolding. At one stage in 1979, Kearney contacted the Department of Health and arranged a visit to the community by a senior official. Little came of it. Several years later, however, the same official — in comments to me — observed that department officials had mistakenly deferred to health board management. Their accounts of what was unfolding minimised and downplayed the problem. Looking back, the official recognised that the department should have had a mechanism in place to respond more quickly to the information being provided by local residents and locally-based professionals. It exposed, the official opined, a major weakness in health board structures. The belated admission was a serious understatement of what had already turned into a catastrophic failure.

Meanwhile, health board management expressed anger that contact had been made with the Department of Health and questioned Kearney's community role and her support for the Development Committee. She changed jobs shortly afterwards. By then some young people had become parents and were coming to the attention of other health board social workers and public health nurses due to child welfare concerns. Some young mothers using heroin were self-referring to the service while others were referred by their parents, now grandparents. Occasionally, it was reported that mothers were pressurised by male friends to use their flats as a base for making drug sales or that there was injecting behaviour in the presence of young children. Some young women pleaded pregnancy to help male partners get non-custodial sentences.[16] It was also reported that mothers 'took the rap' — owned up — for partners' drug supplies seized during Garda raids, with the belief — not always realised — that because they were mothers they would be treated more leniently by the police and the courts. When risks seriously escalated, some children were taken into statutory care. The practice became commonplace as more young heroin-users bore children without changing their risky, precarious lifestyles.

At the time, there was little insight for dealing competently with these situations. As social workers, we were unfamiliar with the impact of parental heroin dependency on children's welfare and there was an inadequate, internal professional support system for assessing new problems or new issues. The monitoring role was highly stressful. As we rarely knew the levels of drug use or drug-dealing involved, our relationships with parents were often volatile and mostly embedded in suspicion, especially as what we saw as support-monitoring, was often, quite reasonably, perceived as unwarranted surveillance.

We were encouraged to seek advice from addiction service experts and this often proved unhelpful as they lacked insight into child welfare issues, and operated from a very narrow addiction perspective. Some drug treatment personnel tended to view child protection simplistically. They argued that because they had a drug dependence, parents needed to be separated from their children for prolonged periods — with court orders — while they underwent unspecified treatment. The executive chairman of the leading drugs treatment centre, Coolmine Therapeutic Community — a voluntary service set up in 1973 by philanthropist Lord Paddy Rossmore — advocated the need for separation, a particularly contentious proposal given that under the Children Act, 1908 (UK) drug-using parents could become subject to fit person orders.[17] The fact that it took a further ten years before Ireland's legislators enacted their own children's legislation was in itself a damning statement about the state's then general lack of attention to children's welfare.

This punitive, leverage approach was naive, unworkable and potentially unethical. There was no available evidence to suggest long periods in treatment, however defined, would make a difference to a parent's drug use let alone their parenting. The approach, moreover, lacked insight into the negative impacts on children of being separated from parents and placed into state care potentially exacerbating their risk and experience of trauma. In general, most social workers considered it better to work with the parents and other concerned adults in mitigating the risks and improve parents' and others' capacities to support the children if possible.

The leverage narrative appealed to those caught up in seeking solutions to child welfare and other problems that otherwise seemed intractable. It was tempting to believe parental abstention from drugs was an answer. Tellingly, there was no clamour for this approach to be used with parents with equivalent or worse alcohol-misuse problems equally damaging to their children.

Terrie Kearney's successor, Patricia Daly, had similar experiences of management stonewalling. She succeeded, nonetheless, in making progress on developing an official response. Daly nurtured a positive relationship with the area's director of community care — a public health doctor — and initiated a proposal for a service with a youth intervention focus. This was referred to as the Youth Development Programme (YDP). When Daly left her position a year later in 1981 to undertake further study, it fell to me as her community worker replacement to develop the YDP.

My early meetings with health management officials about this were not encouraging. Their language on medical oversight was at odds with the written proposal's focus on outreach, youth engagement and community-based interventions. Moreover, there was no evidence that the health board had engaged with other state agencies. While education, training and justice authorities were referenced in the YDP documentation and discussions, no representatives from these statutory bodies were present at health management meetings. Nor was there any evidence that they had been approached at inter-agency management levels.

Health board leadership was conservative, traditionalist, patriarchal and, as I discovered, some members were personally suspicious of social workers. A telling comment was a claim by the most senior official present, second only to the chief executive officer. He said that previously when problems arose in the flat complexes a financial grant was given, usually to a religious order, to assign a nun to operate a service and get on with it. He expressed surprise that the same could not be done now. It was a hankering back to the 'good old days' when the church and religious orders ran everything.

Senior officials preferred these old models, it seemed. They liked the idea of farming out services to religious third parties and for these to be hidden away, whatever the cost. From their perspective, it meant they could manage from a distance, away from the frontline, without taking responsibility for everyday operations. The problems were being dealt with and they were safe in the belief that the religious 'knew' what they were doing and would absorb people's concerns and dissatisfactions as they were rarely challenged.

After my first meeting with the Development Committee, I was shown around the estate. The autumnal dusk had a slight chill and the scene reminded me so much of the communal street life I had witnessed in other public estates, particularly Ballyfermot. Even though darkness beckoned, the estate was full of activity with children gathered under the streetlights after their evening meal. Some played football and chasing while others sat around or walked from one flat to another, poking each other, generally having fun and filling the evening air with their conversation and laughter. Groups of adults gathered to go and play bingo in the nearby National Stadium. Meanwhile, there was an air of excitement after a soccer international at Lansdowne Road where a few local people worked as stewards: Ireland had beaten France in a World Cup qualifying match.

A group of young people assembled at the estate entrance, referred to as Moore's corner, beside a pharmacy of that name. When I passed by later, it was clear some were acquiring, using and selling drugs. They were alert to strangers, their movements furtive and a few were obviously inebriated. I had a sense that with or without drugs, the pharmacy corner was a natural physical space for young people to assemble, have a bit of a laugh, flirt and plan whatever else they might do for the evening. It was a familiar scene in most estates, young people agreeing a place to assemble and hang out, sometimes with alcohol.

At this stage, the pharmacy scene did not seem too exceptional, but with more prolonged and regular observation it was obvious that drug selling had become ubiquitous and open. A continuous stream of people came and went to purchase drugs, gradually moving deeper into the complex to do deals yet still in public view. As time progressed, the numbers increased and eventually a socially threatening atmosphere could be observed. From a conventional perspective, those involved in this drug scene could be deemed, to use a word often applied to such behaviour, chaotic.

Closer observations and discussions, however, revealed they were mostly attached to their lifestyle which clearly had everyday routines and challenges. While their position might easily be described as clueless, such labelling belies an internal, well-defined common purpose (alternative local economy) and social identity (alternative work), even though it exposed them to significant health-related problems, as well as criminality. As observed in a description of heroin users in the classic 1960s New York study: 'They [heroin users] are actively engaged in meaningful activities and relationships seven days a week' and most of the time they are 'aggressively pursuing a career that is exacting, challenging, adventurous, and rewarding'.[18]

Following introductions by the Development Committee's chairperson Paul Humphrey I gradually built up rapport with a small group of younger

The Harm Done

members of this drug-using group. Over time I had several discussions with them about their background involvement and began to develop a picture of their predicament and circumstances. A key moment in their collective story was when a leading drug supplier, a member of the Dunne family known as Boyo, moved into the flats. He established it as a new base for receiving stolen goods: jewellery, cheque books, credit cards and passports. He formed good relationships with young people and often met them in a nearby pub where together they drank and sometimes smoked cannabis. The pub acquired a reputation for customer drug dealing, and was often referred to as the Pharmacy. It eventually closed during the 1990s, never to re-open.

In the pub young people were introduced to Palfium (dextromoramide) and Diconal (dipipanone hydrochloride), powerful synthetic opiates used for severe pain management. The Palfium supply was reportedly from a major break-in at a pharmaceutical warehouse while Diconal was recirculated from medical prescriptions. A culture of injecting rapidly developed with younger people learning the practice from the few older ones who injected drugs (amphetamines) previously in much the same way they would have learned about other teenage activities.[19]

After the Palfium supply dried up, they virtually all switched to heroin. In the early 1980s, a single dose of heroin had a street market price of IR£10, a 500% increase on the price paid for Palfium. It was equivalent to the weekly individual rent in a shared private house or small bedsit, or the price of twenty pints of stout or beer. At IR£2, the Palfium was relatively affordable compared to alcohol. With heroin, the cost surged and it was financially difficult to sustain the habit.

Inevitably, young people's interactions centred around obtaining money for drugs through small-time criminal activities: handbag snatching, mugging, and shop jump-overs. They acquired and exchanged information with other drug users and frequently became small-time dealers themselves. Having been drawn into heroin use, they became vital cogs in its wider distribution to the point that it became impossible to make a distinction between those who only used drugs and those who were also dealers.

Although there were common threads to their lifestyles, it was evident they had individual motivations and reasons to continue with heroin. Some I met had used just a few times and then quickly stopped, managing not to get caught up in the drug scene. They had been successfully diverted by being part of things considered relatively normal and were engaged in activities organised by Development Committee volunteers.

For continuing users, however, several background issues contributed to and exacerbated matters such as the death of a parent or parental conflict or separation. Some stated they were in families with serious alcohol problems. Others joked about being given out to for their drug use by an alcoholic parent. Two alleged they had been sexually abused as children and more said they experienced physical abuse. Virtually all had difficult school experiences with poor records of attendance and an overwhelming sense of exclusion and non-engagement with education.

One group member had spent time in a reformatory. Others had outstanding court charges. A few said they used heroin for thrills, pure and simple. Drug use by others lacked background explanations and appeared random: they were in the wrong place at the wrong time, just as the use of Palfium and then heroin commenced. Most of the group presented as being socially stuck, as having perhaps inadvertently got involved in something that had completely engulfed them. They found it difficult, if not impossible, to escape.

The three principal dealers — linked to Boyo's network — used heroin. Despite their visible wealth, like most others involved, they also had troubling backgrounds. Virtually all then-known dealers had had difficult childhoods and experienced considerable trauma and illness as they got older. All died prematurely. Lower-level dealers had visibility, but more in terms of being able to buy and sell consumer goods or in financially supporting family members rather than in outward displays of wealth or fortune.

The problem had a significant impact on community life, upsetting previously accepted norms on interdependence. The financial rewards for becoming involved in dealing and extended activities were difficult to resist. For a while, so many people were either directly or indirectly involved it was hard to know who for sure was or was not. This caused people to retreat from engaging openly with neighbours lest they find out too much or get caught up in dealing themselves.

At one stage, Boyo approached the local priest offering to donate several food parcels for the 'poor' at Christmas. While this bizarre offer was rejected, it underlined rapidly changing community relations. Overall, there was a great deal of suspicion and a pervasive fear. Any trust previously taken for granted was deeply undermined.

Knowing that heroin use was continuing to rise, the Development Committee, in September 1981, conducted a research exercise of a type now described in sociology as popular epidemiology. The approach involves individuals or groups without formal qualifications in research

The Harm Done

sciences finding a way to count people believed to have a health or social problem and to establish a prevalence statistic for that problem within the group or locality.

The approach is useful in detecting problems that are clustered together as distinct from those randomly distributed in the general population. It borrows greatly from the seminal work of John Snow (1813–58), known as the father of epidemiology. Through assiduous foot slogging, Snow traced the origins of a cholera outbreak in Soho, London, to a particular water supply. He later halted the outbreak by making arrangements for breaking the handle of a pump in Broad Street where today there is a plaque in his memory.

In the instance of the St Teresa's Gardens Development Committee's research on heroin, a sub-group of committee members mapped out each flat from a total of three-hundred-and-forty. They recorded the number of persons at each address, the number known by them to be using heroin and the number under sixteen living in the same households. At the time sixteen was the legal cut-off between child and adult. The results caused surprise, not so much by the total number but by the pattern of concentration.

The overall number of people using heroin was estimated at sixty-three, or 5% of the total population of 1,260.[20] Forty-four families had at least one person who actively used heroin which was 13% of the total number of units. All except ten of those using heroin were under twenty-five, one was twelve having started heroin when he was nine. Twenty per cent of those aged 15–24, were identified as using heroin. This estimate rose to 35% for the male age cohort. Fifty-six per cent of those thought to be using were from sixteen family units, and in three families alone each had three young persons involved. In all, over one hundred separate children — over 8% of the total population — were living in family environments considered to be high social risk because of parental and / or sibling heroin use.[21]

It was an extraordinary result. Later research undertaken by a team from the Royal College of Surgeons — led by Fergus O'Kelly and his colleague Gerard Bury — came to an even higher estimate of eighty-one persons from sixty-three families.[22] Their study took in the wider electoral ward area, but outside of St Teresa's Gardens they could identify, within the ward, only one additional heroin user. In making sense of its own information the Development Committee assumed, based on personal testimonies, that most people they knew to be taking heroin shared injecting equipment. The number of younger siblings, over one hundred

— all living in the same family situations — was deeply troubling.

In addition to this local survey, figures for those seeking opiate addiction treatment during 1979–83 were, a few years later, rearranged by the NDATC in its analysis into 16 electoral ward groupings in Dublin City.[23] The data show that in 1981, the number attending from the St Teresa's Gardens grouping — the St Teresa's Gardens area ward and two other adjacent ward areas — constituted an attendance rate of 604 persons per 100,000 population. This was more than two-and-a-half times the next highest per head of population figure of 222 from an electoral ward grouping in the north inner city. By 1983, the respective per head of population figures for both groupings had risen to 736 and 471. The lowest recorded rate within the-then Dublin City boundary was 28 in the northeastern suburb of Howth, a ratio of 26:1 between the highest and lowest ward groupings.

At this latter stage, 67% (621) of NDATC clients from within Dublin City (928) — not including county areas such as Ballymun, Clondalkin, Dún Laoghaire and Tallaght — came from six of the sixteen electoral ward groupings in the city. They included the low income communities of Ballyfermot, Finglas, north inner city and south inner city. These four areas alone accounted for 47% of the total of all persons (city, county and rest of Ireland) seeking opiate treatment in 1983. This pattern and its supporting evidence strongly suggested that heroin use was concentrated in areas of deep social disadvantage. But it suited neither the political nor the administrative / clinical narratives of the day to draw attention to this. While the Development Committee's information was submitted to a newly appointed internal health board committee on drugs, which convened in early 1982, it had little impact on health board management.

Dublin's growing drug problem during the early 1980s was eventually taken up by local politicians and councillors, some of whom were hearing of and dealing with drug-related representations in their clinics. In October 1981, a special meeting of Dublin City Council discussed the matter.[24] I was asked by the Fine Gael lord mayor, Sen Alexis Fitzgerald Jnr (1945–2015), through the director of community care, to make a brief presentation. In this I referred to the problem's correlation with housing, unemployment and other factors. I was taken aback by the presentations from some health officials who minimised the problem, suggesting matters were in hand.

Afterwards, the lord mayor requested a copy of my presentation which he then brought to a follow-up meeting with the city manager, the health board's chief executive and other senior officials. Health officials

The Harm Done

were angry that the document had not been processed through their internal structures before being tabled at this level. Although they had been at the council meeting, they berated my immediate superiors for the 'embarrassment' caused to them. My superiors in turn berated me. The director of community care explained that everybody up the food chain had got their knuckles rapped, his included. As a result he had to do the same to me and to instruct the senior social worker to do likewise.

Though comical, the episode was also a dreadful reflection on the health board's defensiveness and state of paranoia. Following this encounter, a decision was taken nonetheless to move ahead in a practical sense and develop the proposed Youth Development Programme. A partnership group consisting of community representatives and personnel from education, primary care, general medical practice, social work and probation services was appointed to steer and give local direction to the project. A highly qualified social work practitioner, then based in Scotland, uprooted to join as project leader in July 1982 and knuckled down. But she quickly realised that health board management were neither willing nor able to keep momentum going. Key aspects of project implementation were making little headway. This included, for example, a failure to secure and refurbish a nearby standalone premises that had been made available and for which the Department of Health had promised funding.

Moreover, a withdrawal of funding for the recruitment of two outreach staff was apparent amid claims that resources previously targeted for the YDP had been diverted for political expediency to projects in other catchment areas. Eventually, out of frustration with foot-dragging and a perceived lack of genuine commitment, the project leader resigned in April 1983, nine months after her appointment. In an open letter to health board management and much to their embarrassment, she made clear her reasons. She said she found it impossible to reconcile her position with the fact that no advancement of the proposed project had happened in the previous seven months. It seemed to her that it would not get off the ground due to apparent lack of commitment by the health board and lack of finance. The resignation was a huge blow to the YDP committee and to prospects for developing a locally-based partnership response.

Earlier in 1982, other factors began to have an impact on political attitudes towards the drug issue. Following the February general election (see Chapter 2), the balance of power in the Dáil was held by independent north inner city TD Tony Gregory. In exchange for his support — abstaining from the vote to elect a Taoiseach — Gregory secured key policy concessions on inner city issues and had regular access to Government ministers with whom he could raise matters of emerging interest. During one such meeting with Health Minister Michael Woods TD, Gregory and his advisers flagged the escalating drug problem in his constituency just as local professionals and community and youth workers in the south inner city were raising these matters during community discussions.

Woods later engaged the director of the Medico-Social Research Board (MSRB), Geoffrey Dean (1918–2009), to ascertain the evidence to support Gregory's claims about problem heroin use in the city. This approach was viewed externally as the minister seeking a way around his own senior health officials who disputed the view that there was a serious problem. Dean commissioned a scoping study from a retired independent public health expert, John Bradshaw. He undertook a three-day inquiry, meeting representatives from several relevant agencies, such as the Garda Síochána, the health board, Coolmine and NDATC. He also met me, the YDP project leader, members of the local Development Committee and others working on the ground in the north / south city areas and parts of Ballymun and Dún Laoghaire.

Bradshaw appeared distressed during and after his meetings. His emotive July 1982 report described the problem as an epidemic that may have been created by a 'profound sickness in society'. Appalled that the problem was gripping young people so quickly in a few poor communities, he saw it was likely to spread to other similar areas.

The following year the MSRB published a more in-depth study of heroin use in the north inner city undertaken by Bradshaw. In this he cited the difficulty of trying to convince policymakers that the problem existed in the manner he had previously described. In this latter study he referred to the earlier report, stating: 'A number of persons, worthy of respect, expressed the view that the various supposed addicts and those trying to help them locally had, perhaps unwittingly, greatly exaggerated the problem, and so therefore had the report'.[25]

Bradshaw had hoped to conduct a comparable in depth study in St Teresa's Gardens as he knew the estimates of heroin users there were higher than elsewhere. But local community members and community-based professionals decided not to facilitate this study for a number of reasons including that from their viewpoint, adequate information had already been provided to the health authorities. The most that could be achieved by another study was that Bradshaw might discover a few more than those already identified. In addition to the Development Committee's epidemiological research, several community-based professionals,

The Harm Done

doctors, nurses and social workers, had provided substantial corroborative accounts.

Bradshaw was clearly disappointed about this and stated to local representatives that their information would not be believed because it lacked the independent verification his research could supply. But people from the St Teresa's Gardens Development Committee were reluctant to raise expectations by participating further in research. They retorted that they doubted he would be believed either. At the time they were somewhat embittered following the YDP project leader's resignation and the reasons given and the obvious lack of progress in the YDP's development. They remained unconvinced that Bradshaw's efforts would make much of a difference to official attitudes.

After the collapse of the Gregory-supported Government in November 1982, a new Fine Gael / Labour coalition (1982–87) established the Special Government Task Force on Drug Abuse in April 1983. This consisted of junior ministers who would consider Bradshaw's reports and the drug issue more widely. The Development Committee and other local groups made submissions to the task force. The Government subsequently withheld the task force's main 1983 finding and recommendation. It specified that disadvantaged areas should be prioritised and designated for a targeted youth and community response. The report went unpublished. Instead, a press statement on the findings excluded all references to this key recommendation. The extent of institutional denial was deeper than anything previously suspected.

Entrance to the National Drug Advisory and Treatment Centre located in a prefabricated building, at corner of Jervis Street Hospital, early-1980s
Photo: Paul Humphrey Collection.

Nancy Reagan during her visit to Daytop Village, N.Y., on Oct. 23, 1980
(AP Photo/Suzanne Vlamis). Courtesy: Alamy ©

CHAPTER 4

Abstinence Model for Managing Drug Problems

When I took up a community work role in the south inner city the dominant public discourse about drug issues was simplistic. It did not distinguish between opiates and cocaine, on the one hand, and cannabis on the other. There was no mention at all of alcohol as a drug. At Trinity College cannabis was widely consumed in the Buttery bar, rooms and on the grass verges around the cricket pitch. Drug issues never featured as a topic in lectures or tutorials. The only reference to drugs from a lecturer that I can recall was from Noreen Kearney when she presented a case study of a young woman in a family struggling to make ends meet. She later commented that the mother 'had been heard to say that if she could have the cash value of the anti-depressant drugs she is prescribed, she would not need them because she would have enough money to buy food'.[1] It was a telling reflection on the impact of poverty on struggling families.

At the time, there were well-established differences internationally in how drug problems were conceptualised and managed. In the US, whose policies had aggressive global reach, these problems were perceived primarily in terms of crime. For over six decades after it was passed, the Harrison Narcotic Act (1914) was interpreted as allowing the prosecuting of medical professionals who prescribed opiates for the treatment of addiction.[2] After Ronald Reagan was inaugurated as US president in 1981, the so-called War on Drugs — which was first declared by President Richard Nixon in 1971 — was escalated. In a somewhat softer style, First Lady Nancy Reagan embarked on her naïve Just Say No campaign aimed at schoolchildren.[3] By combining war rhetoric with that of individual weakness, the policing of poor communities became more militarised while drug-taking in the same communities was represented as 'the consequence of collective personal failure'[4] — the poor simply needed to learn how to say No.

Nancy Reagan's interest in drugs followed her visit to Daytop Village — a therapeutic community founded in 1963 based in New York City and currently merged with Samaritan Daytop Village— during the presidential election. The original Daytop model for alcohol / drug treatment derives from a mental health mutual self- help movement. In therapeutic communities patients and therapists live together in a user-led, staff-supported therapeutic environment in which active user-participation is promoted.[5] When first established in mental health services, therapeutic communities were viewed as a form of liberation, an attempt to move patient care towards a more open, democratic treatment. Participants played a direct role in their own and others' treatment. In a residential setting, the focus was on building a therapeutic structure free from over-arching external influence. When residents learned new tools in responsibility and decision-making they were then able to move from the community back into society.[6]

Psychiatrist R.D. Laing, who co-founded the Philadelphia Association, to challenge established ways of thinking about and responding to distress'[7], revelled in experimental psychiatry and set up Kingsley Hall — a 'sprawling house' that 'became an asylum in the original Greek sense of the word: a refuge, a safe haven for the psychotic and the schizophrenic, where there were no locks on the doors and no anti-psychotic drugs were administered' and where people 'were free to come and go as they pleased'.[8]

Nancy Reagan revisited Daytop after her husband took office to discuss a role for herself in a wider campaign. Daytop, reflecting a US - UK divide on these matters, was a lot more structured than Laing's somewhat anarchic model. She was obviously impressed with Daytop's emphasis on peer support and peer education in an overall personal responsibility framework. Although prevention programmes based on her Just Say No mantra became popular in US media, school managements and among politicians it eventually became discredited. It was widely regarded — from evaluative research — as counter-productive[9], and basically feeding young people's interest in drug experimentation.[10] Moreover, it reinforced the populist uninformed idea that young people could be shocked into resisting drug taking by simply telling them the awful facts'[11] or by sending drug offenders to schools giving talks about the effects.[12]

The Irish education authorities, to their credit, have long since adopted the more creditable life skills approach to school-based drug prevention. This was despite efforts by Daytop advocates in Ireland to introduce prevention campaigns based on the War on Drugs rhetoric. The 1983 launch of a campaign to train Lions Club[13] members throughout Ireland in how to form parent support groups was naively informed that the campaign's ultimate aim was to 'establish a drug free environment in which young people can grow up without the threat of drug abuse'.[14]

As well as therapeutic communities such as Daytop Village, the Alcoholics Anonymous mutual self-help fellowships, including Narcotics Anonymous, were drawn from by those who conceptualised drug problems as disease. The fellowships, started in the US in the 1930s and expanded enormously over the next nine decades, were never intended to promote any specific model of addiction. Fundamentally, they were mutual support groups where people assembled without precondition other than they owned their addiction and aspired to achieving sobriety.

While not constituting formal treatment per se, the fellowships had huge importance in helping millions of people worldwide to develop and maintain a focus on being alcohol and drug free. Unfortunately, self-selecting peer-support groups do not lend themselves to classic research enquiry and while participation is huge it is virtually impossible to assess their effectiveness. There is a body of literature however that supports their value in complementing other formal treatment programmes.[15] In general those who participate in fellowships while undertaking professional treatment do better than those who do not. The more intense their involvement and attendance the better they do, with more evidence of abstinence over the medium to long term.[16]

Numerous specialist addiction programmes — most notably the so called Minnesota Model — incorporate fellowship principles (referred to as the twelve steps[17]) into their treatment regimes. The Minnesota Model was formally established in Center City, Minnesota in 1949. It fuses AA with ideas from therapeutic communities, thereby creating a professional structure to help people develop a lifetime commitment to abstinence and dedication to AA attendance. Although influenced by AA's twelve steps, the Minnesota Model is separate. It is commonly organised through an intensive post-detoxification, four- to six-week residential programme or combined hospital detoxification and residential. Treatment methods include individual and group therapy, educational sessions and active participation in the residential community.[18] Outside the Minnesota Model, the AA components are open to anybody irrespective of their compliance with the rules of formal treatment.

It is contended by disease model protagonists that people with this condition can recover provided they adhere to a relevant formally prescribed programme, either Minnesota Model or similar, and by abstaining from all drugs and alcohol. The therapy is underpinned by an acceptance that addiction exists as a primary condition with spiritual as well as mental and physical effects, all of which need to be addressed for treatment effectiveness. The phrase 'in-recovery' commonly refers to a person who has become abstinent through participating in treatment.

Although the abstinence model as espoused by the various Minnesota-type programmes is popular internationally, it has application only to that small minority of alcohol- and drug-takers who self categorise as addict and who seek recovery in the form of abstinence. In other words, it works for those who develop a belief in it. State services need to allow for non-believers, however. Unfortunately, Irish state services wedded to the abstinence model had no alternatives during the 1980s.

The Mental Treatment Act (1945) defined addicts as 'persons who by reason of their addiction to drink, to drugs or intoxicants were suffering from mental illness'. Following the Act's passing there was a diffusion of the disease model — for alcohol treatment — into psychiatric hospitals. The principles underlying the AA fellowship were incorporated into this work and the first European AA meeting was held in an Irish psychiatric hospital in 1946.[19] In accordance with the legislation people with a drug addiction could be admitted. While a few drug admissions were recorded, in general the addiction focus was exclusively on those dependent on alcohol. Mental health services — open to expanding treatment for alcohol — expressed no interest in illegal drugs.

A specialist service for drug addiction (see Chapter 3), the National Drug Advisory and Treatment Centre (NDATC) — a psychiatry-led multi-disciplinary team — was established in the late 1960s at a prefab annex in Jervis Street Hospital in central Dublin.[20] It offered services exclusively from its hospital base and did not undertake outreach to community locations. The clinic's status as a national specialist centre contrasted with services for people with alcohol problems in the state's network of county psychiatric hospitals. In 1981, for example, the annual number of total admissions to psychiatric hospitals for alcohol disorders, nationally, peaked at almost seven-and-a-half thousand (the number of first admissions peaked the following year at two-thousand-five-hundred-

Abstinence Model for Managing Drug Problems

and-eighteen, or 26% of all first admissions).[21] Meanwhile, the NDATC had access to a closed ward of twelve in-patient detoxification beds, first in the Central Mental Hospital in Dundrum and then in Beaumont Hospital on Dublin's northside.

The relatively liberal open-door access for patients considered through no fault of their own to have alcohol dependence contrasted sharply with the more punitive approach taken towards drug users, although both were treated medically using the same disease model perspective. The drug takers' situation because it was illegal and considered self-inflicted was treated outside of mainstream provision. At its outset, the NDATC incorporated a US-style punitive abstinence ethos. In this way the disease model of treatment, as previously established for alcohol in psychiatric hospitals, was extended as a specialism into the NDATC.

In its first two decades, the NDATC had no long-term methadone treatment, referred to as phy programmes (Physeptone was a form of methadone) and was provided only as a detoxification. To avail of it, those presenting needed to 'prove their sincerity' and have 'some form of motivation and commitment to give up using heroin'. Once detoxified, they would have to avail of psychosocial therapy towards this objective.[22] Physeptone was made available to pregnant women however, to reduce harm to the foetus should the mother continue to use street drugs.[23]

The general physeptone situation became farcical. Many attendees from St Teresa's Gardens, for example, told me they had several episodes of pleading their sincerity to remain abstinent as a convenient way to get a short-term clean drug supply. It gave them an alternative pharmacy for when street and selling activities got overwhelming. Within weeks they were back where they started.

The main psychosocial therapies promoted by the NDATC fused ideas from the NA fellowship, the Minnesota Model and therapeutic communities. Through exposure to group work and counselling, participants were helped to embrace a lifelong abstinence that could be attained and maintained through regular attendance at mutual support groups such as NA and others. More treatment was generally considered better although the NDATC's confined physical spaces were not conducive to intensive treatment. As an alternative, residential treatment was strongly advocated and considered optimal.

The NDATC had close working relations with Coolmine and encouraged many patients to go there for residential rehabilitation.[24] Coolmine had a close association with the Daytop programme. In 1981, Daytop assigned a senior staff member, Sam Anglin to be Coolmine

The Harm Done

director for a short period of reorganisation. A Coolmine graduate, Thomas McGarry, went to Daytop for training and succeeded Anglin on his return.[25] Anglin represented Coolmine on the YDP committee set up in early 1982. He attended meetings until the following August when he returned to the US. Coolmine did not replace him on the YDP.

In an interview with the *Irish Press* at the time Anglin described Coolmine as a 'cross between a fraternity and a kibbutz' and also explained that contrary 'to what most people believe, when an addict takes a drug he's not taking it to get high, he's taking it to make his bad feelings disappear'. He continued: 'What we do here is to instill emotional antibodies in people'.[26]

Prior to Anglin's involvement, I was among those from the YDP committee positively disposed towards Coolmine. At the time it was the only non-governmental organisation that appeared to know anything about drugs from a practice perspective. In general, within mental health the therapeutic community model was viewed positively especially by those who believed, as I did, in self-recovery's democratic ethos. It was assumed this ethos permeated drug therapeutic communities also.

When Coolmine was set up, heroin was not a substantial drug problem in Ireland. For its first few years it struggled greatly to have an impact on other forms of drug use. Following the upsurge in heroin use in the early 1980s, Coolmine underwent significant organisational transformation and after an internal leadership purge facilitated by Anglin, it successfully positioned itself as the dominant addiction therapy exponent and service provider. Reflecting Daytop's influence, it claimed to be ready, willing and able to roll-out Just Say No type prevention schemes with parents and school-going children and to develop an under-eighteen's drug-free recovery programme with schooling attached.[27]

The Coolmine treatment programme could take almost eighteen months to complete. It emphasised psychological restructuring to stop residents being addiction-prone. It helped them reorganise their social lives so they could establish new social networks, free of drugs and other people who used drugs and away from the families and communities in which their drug use started and was sustained.[28] It was described as 'like the creation of a new family for the drug addict where he can go through the maturation process this time without drugs'.[29]

The Coolmine intake assessment included an interview with five to six senior residents alongside a staff representative, during which those seeking entry had to be convincing about their desire for recovery and a 'cure' from addiction. It is also explained that the two basic rules were no drugs and no violence. If the rules were broken, expulsion would follow with no readmission.[30] Given the strictness of assessment it is hardly surprising that in 1982, while the first heroin epidemic was at its gravest mainly in poor communities, Coolmine admissions were biased in favour of the better educated socio-economic groupings.[31] According to Anglin in his *Irish Press* interview, less than 25% of those who were resident at any one time, would in due course, overcome addiction. The level of investment, and time commitment, for such a poor outcome, attracted little media or political comment at the time, or since.

Anglin arranged a study visit to Coolmine for a few members of the YDP committee. In general, the visit went well and senior residents were thorough in explaining the therapy and showing us around the facilities. Two incidents, however, caused discomfort. In the first, we were present in the office when a phone call was answered in an unfriendly, dismissive manner: 'Yes, that's right, ring back tomorrow, same time.' We were told that the person ringing — a male — was being assessed for a place on the programme. To establish motivation, he was requested to ring in daily. A formal assessment would take place only if he rang on successive days at about the same time.

The explanation seemed plausible, except that home telephones were rare during the early 1980s. There were only a few home telephones in St Teresa's Gardens and similar estates. The nearest working public facility was on the South Circular Road, which like other such phones regularly had queues on the pathway outside. The call-in arrangement clearly favoured those who lived in homes that already had a telephone.

The second incident arose while we were in the process of a group discussion with senior residents. Another resident appeared from an adjacent room with a placard around his shoulders on which were written words about him being an adolescent. It was explained that he had failed that morning to complete his room cleaning chores to others' satisfaction. As this failure reflected on them all he was confronted about the matter in group therapy and called out as 'adolescent' whereupon he agreed to wear the placard. On leaving, we were less enthusiastic about the Coolmine model and for sure we resisted Anglin's suggestions — presented somewhat dogmatically — that the YDP should be modelled on its ethos and structures.

After reorganisation Coolmine developed a remarkable media profile. Its main spokesperson was James Comberton who, following the leadership purge, became executive chair. This position combined chair of the management board and chief executive officer — a highly unusual arrangement for a legal entity. He had a public relations background and regularly made buoyant, unsubstantiated claims with little challenge to the value and efficacy of Coolmine's treatment and prevention strategy. In practice, this meant its ethos — like that of the NDATC— of aiming for drug-free, abstinent lifestyles was regularly reinforced publicly as the dominant, practically exclusive, drug treatment approach to be used in Ireland. Internationally, though, the therapeutic community model had little evidential basis for drug treatment.[32]

By dominating the public narrative, Coolmine succeeded in avoiding the burden of proof with the media and others. This included myself and other colleagues. So it had a relatively free rein with little or no critique. At an early stage, it operated a rather harsh regime that was considerably modified since the mid-noughties. The centre since then has adopted evidence-based counselling standards with a high number of its staff trained in community approaches, as described in Chapter 8 and it also now has services for women with children, and works in conjunction with some community drug teams and task forces.[33]

The work of the NDATC and Coolmine enabled the abstinence model to dominate the statutory treatment response to heroin problems at their outset and did so for almost two decades. Coolmine created the National Federation of Community Action on Drugs in which drug use was seen as progressing from 'drinking to hash, to harder drugs and often finally to heroin', an analysis that was contradicted by the then data about heroin use. Although not directly involved in treatment per se, the federation opposed drug substitution therapies and believed rehabilitation could be made easier by the utopian idea of 'ensuring a drug-free society for those who have had treatment'.[34] In the mid 1980s, Coolmine expanded greatly by taking over a former domestic sciences teaching convent — St Martha's — in Navan, Co Meath, and operated a facility with up to 75 residents. But it over-extended itself and a few years after its official opening by the then Health Minister Barry Desmond St Martha's closed permanently with health administrators refusing to underwrite its excessive costs.

In practical terms, the abstinence model was useful to only a minority of drug-takers and, it had no relevance whatsoever for those not seeking abstinence but who were simply seeking help in managing their continued drug use and related problems. The model's key philosophy could potentially, be viewed as suited to particular societies with a can-do, individualist ethos. The fact that the model dominated treatment in US society was no basis for having it rolled out elsewhere, and it certainly seemed inexplicable that Irish policy-makers looked more to the US disease model than to Europe or the UK — which operated a more rational system — especially as in staffing terms the NDATC appeared to be modelled on the UK's clinic system (see Chapter 8).

Despite significant changes in the operation of services since the late 1990s, the abstinence model continues to be represented as the ideal.[35] It is instructive that drug-free recovery typifies the optimal desired outcome from Government investment — supported across several political viewpoints — at times leading people who self-declare they are in recovery being placed on a pedestal. This potentially leaves them unnecessarily carrying unrealistic, public and media expectations. Meanwhile those who continue to use controlled drugs with various efforts at integration are occasionally viewed as lacking aspiration.

Barry Cullen and John Moylan during rehearsals for the Fighting Back drama, March 1983.
Photo: Paul Humphrey Collection

Summer Project, St Teresa's Gardens early 1980s.
Photo: Tony O'Shea ©

CHAPTER 5

A Community Fights Back

In addition to helping form the Youth Development Project in 1981–82, as community social worker I worked alongside community groups in the south inner city to organise public information meetings. Topics covered were foster care, social welfare benefits, housing maintenance and drugs. Housing meetings in St Teresa's Gardens during early 1981 led to a concerted campaign by residents for physical improvements, especially after flooding of water drains and problems arising from waste collections. In March 1982 residents had a public meeting and walkabout with local politicians — including Ben Briscoe TD (1934–2023) from Fianna Fáil and Cllr Dan Browne from Labour (nd – 2010). A second public meeting on April 29 1982 coincided with the launch by the development committee of a one-off publication The Gardens. It provided an opportunity to outline more specific concerns and also managed to get media coverage.[1]

Drug meetings throughout the area followed a similar standard format. For instance, one held in May 1981 in the Little Flower Community Centre, Meath Street, consisted of outside 'expert' speakers invited to present and respond to people's queries. About 100 people attended, including politicians. Denis Mullins who headed the Garda Drugs Squad spoke of his delight in seeing local groups organise community meetings. He considered them a significant development in tackling drug issues. A Coolmine representative followed who highlighted family upbringing as the main cause of heroin use. The solution to the problem lay in love, care and knowing where the children were, who they were with and what they were doing. A National Drug Advisory and Treatment Centre (NDATC) speaker detailed drug types, effects, chemical properties and symptoms of illicit use.

The Harm Done

When each speaker finished, they were politely applauded. After about sixty minutes the chairperson opened the meeting to the floor. There was a blank silence. Eventually one woman asked: 'What about the pushers?' Even more silence. 'I mean, what are you going to do about the pushers?' she continued. 'There are pushers here in this hall and I know them.' Another woman said that at a previous meeting she had named a dealer. The next day she, not the pusher, was raided by the gardaí who said they were looking for drugs and guns. The way she saw it pushers were 'king' and so powerful they could organise Garda raids on local people who stood up to them. The meeting persisted in this angry, bewildered vein for some time.

A few people said the gardaí appeared to have little difficulty stopping, searching and harassing young people while the drug dealers were given a free rein. Some women said they were parents of teenage children who were injecting heroin. They expressed an overwhelming sense of confusion, anger and frustration at not being able to cope with a problem they had never experienced. It was not, they said, that they did not love their children or know the inherent risks associated with alcohol and drug use. They had shown their love for them in the same way they had their older brothers and sisters, but they had never had to deal with heroin.

This discussion was repeated at other meetings throughout the area, including in Rialto (Dolphin House and Fatima Mansions) and St Teresa's Gardens. Each event had over 100 people attending and it became apparent that invited speakers could not provide answers to people's basic concerns about why there was so much drug-dealing and drug use in their communities. And, that apart from constantly searching young people, the authorities seemed to be doing little about it. They were not looking for lectures on the origins of chemical substances and their physiological and psychological effects. Some present were upset at the suggestion they might not love their children enough.

They wanted explanations to help relieve the anxiety and fear that had built up over time. The main dealers had a wide network of associates, including people at the meetings, who derived considerable benefit from drug-related activities. They were hardly going to let their business be undermined. It was inevitable that residents felt intimidated.

One public meeting organised by my colleague Patricia Daly in St Teresa's Gardens in early 1981, resulted in an ongoing family support group being set up. It began to meet as parents, mainly mothers, continued to seek support and explanations for their children's drug use. The local drug dealer issue was duly raised and, as with previous meetings, some later regretted doing so. The drug dealers and others in their network had heard back from the meetings. They reportedly intimidated those who spoke up against them.

Days before a scheduled meeting in this series in June 1981, a few local youths overdosed on a batch of heroin and became quite sick. Anger was widespread and the parents' meeting provided an opportunity to channel these concerns. Some of the fifty or so present wanted to tackle the alleged drug dealers there and then. As the situation became volatile, one guest speaker, Frank Deasy (1959–2009) from the Ballymun Youth Action Project, defused the anger by suggesting a delegation should bring forward a petition previously prepared for the Minister for Health (At the time the Minister for Health was Michael Woods, from Fianna Fáil but was replaced on June 30 1981 by Eileen Desmond [1932–2005] from Labour). An accompanying public statement should highlight the lack of an official response from the minister.

The statement, issued a few weeks later in August, garnered media coverage. One resident was quoted as saying they had considered taking the law into their own hands but had feared a bloodbath — mostly their own blood.[2] The comment was telling. Residents' fears of being targeted by the dealers resulted in the drug campaign losing impetus. Parent support meetings came to an end. For almost two years, there were no further such meetings in St Teresa's Gardens. The pattern was repeated in other communities such as Meath Street, Rialto and elsewhere. Initial once-off public meetings were well supported, but interest waned when the focus shifted to drug dealing and how dealers might be tackled. The main dealers were untouchable, it appeared, and could not be assailed.

In 1982, members of St Teresa's Gardens Development Committee undertook a full-time community leadership course funded mainly through the national training authority, then known as AnCO (An Chomhairle Oiliúna). In my community worker role, I was to coordinate the programme. As well as building skills and knowledge, the course gave the committee opportunities to network with more organised groups elsewhere and so improve capacities for dealing with Government agencies and media. Their extensive house-to-house survey provided useful information on local issues and problems.

During training, the group prepared a short drama called Fighting Back. They presented it to an invited audience when they completed the course and later presented it in the local youth centre. The drama told the fictional story of a couple recently returned from Birmingham who moved into the flat complex. Both got involved in developing local activities in

The Harm Done

tackling problems around the maintenance of the flats. Eventually, after a succession of failures, forgotten promises and a growing frustration with the impact of the drug problem, they became disillusioned and sought a new life by transferring to a council house in the suburbs.

Although fictional, Fighting Back was an all-too-familiar story for residents saddened by the rate at which community members were leaving out of frustration with the drug problem and other developments. The drama, imbued with humour, portrayed their plight as a mix of individual, family and communal tragedy. Written and performed by the community members themselves, it had an immense impact on the local audience. They could easily relate to the issues sketched out before them. Perhaps most significantly, the drama was followed by an open debate.

During these discussions, the drug issue returned in sharp focus. Since the previous wave of meetings two years earlier, the dealers had expanded their market. Not only were they supplying a larger population in their own and nearby communities, they were selling to several hundred outsiders and other dealers who, according to local accounts, were arriving at St Teresa's Gardens in a continuous flow of cars and taxis.

Parents who had been at the previous family support meetings started to meet again and expressed an interest in doing something more substantial. They were mindful that previous attempts to raise the drugs issue had generated fear and subsequently faltered. Now, with a renewed community interest inspired by Fighting Back, they showed greater confidence. But they remained unclear about the type and form of action needed. While they spoke about confronting the dealers, they did little about it. Nonetheless, they were prepared to continue meeting to discuss the issue, and seemed unafraid about the prospects of intimidation.

In May 1983, RTÉ's current affairs programme Today Tonight tackled Dublin's heroin problems. The report, produced on the back of John Bradshaw's recently published account of drugs in the north inner city, included a sequence on St Teresa's Gardens. The complex was filmed from a helicopter and a bedroom window in the nearby Coombe Hospital. It was portrayed as a no-go depraved place and described by a young female with a posh south Dublin accent as an area where heroin was most freely available.

Watching in their homes, St Teresa's Gardens residents were hurt and infuriated at how this comment was broadcast and with the disregard shown to their community. Community members were interested, however, in the coverage of drug problems in Hardwicke Street flats on the city's northside. After dealers moved into that area, a local committee with priest Jim Smyth and a Sinn Féin community activist Christy Burke, confronted them. They asked them either to stop dealing or leave the community. The dealers packed up and left.

Hardwicke Street residents accused RTÉ of unbalanced coverage of this incident. They argued that the state broadcaster had attributed too much importance to Burke's Sinn Féin membership and, by extension, the party's IRA links. Although Burke was previously active in the IRA, he was well known for his activism and service on behalf of local people. Indeed, he was initially at pains to point out that his engagement with the drugs issue had nothing to do with his political involvement. Notwithstanding Burke's affiliations, many people from St Teresa's Gardens saw the action of Hardwicke Street residents as a model for what was needed in their own community. They decided to organise a public meeting to stop their own drug dealing issue.

The meeting was held a few weeks later. About fifty people attended. It was relatively calm and openly focused on four alleged drug dealers, whether and how they should be warned to stop their activities. During the evening a delegation visited the named individuals to convey the meeting's views. They returned to report that three of the four individuals were at home and had agreed to stop. The meeting then focused on how to monitor the arrangement. It was decided to keep all drug dealers under surveillance and maintain pressure on them by holding further meetings. An anti-drugs committee was not formed on the basis that other community members would abrogate individual responsibility to stay focused on the problem. That night people approaching the flats complex looking for supplies were turned away. Perimeter patrols were organised by roster and arrangements were made with taxi companies to drop passengers at the estate's only entrance.

These actions caused an overnight crisis in Dublin's heroin supply. While the Hardwicke Street action had effectively established the practice of an organised community confronting drug dealers in its vicinity, the dealers had a relatively small market with little significant impact on the city's overall supply. St Teresa's Gardens, on the other hand, was a well-established central point of supply for most of south Dublin and beyond. News of St Teresa's Gardens spread rapidly to the city's drug using population and the services that worked with them. In my office, colleagues called me with reports that people had difficulties getting their drugs.

Meanwhile, the move gathered momentum as more residents signed up for patrol shifts. They brought a few people to the NDATC and helped to arrange treatments. Other users, encouraged by the extent of the popular response, decided to go cold turkey. Many who decided to use these options during summer 1983 later managed to stay off opiates. Some are still alive today as a result. Even more significant was the impact on younger cohorts who might otherwise have started to use heroin, but did not. Community actions leadership training, anti-drug actions, and the opening of youth and counselling services were seen, alongside Garda actions in limiting supply, as contributing to the observed fall in the number of first-time heroin users in the area from 1982.[3]

Public meetings grew in numbers and additional unwritten aims and rules were formulated. Distinctions were made between users and dealers, the latter having amassed visible personal wealth. Since most of the former were also low-level dealers, this distinction was not always clear cut. Procedures were adopted to deal with allegations of drug dealing. It was agreed that residents would try to protect people making allegations with testimony at public meetings, even if these were then shown to be unfounded. By contrast, there would be no protection for those who made allegations outside of these agreed parameters.

'Protection of the people' as this was framed underlined a willingness to stand together at meetings to examine and assess allegations of heroin dealing only. An early attempt, for example, to raise issues about a sex-worker allegedly using a local flat for business was roundly rejected on the basis that these claims were completely outside the remit of meetings. Similarly, it was agreed that cannabis dealing would not be discussed. This contrasted with the situation two years earlier when those who spoke up at public meetings later felt isolated and intimidated.

It was decided that allegations of drug dealing needed to be backed up at public meetings by reliable testimony from former friends or colleagues of dealers with information on actual recent sales. Once testimonies were given, alleged dealers if present could respond. If they were absent, they were requested to attend the next meeting. If they then failed to turn up, the matter was dealt with in their absence. This rarely happened as in most instances alleged dealers attended these meetings. Sometimes, they admitted they were dealers. When dealing was denied they were questioned by residents and often during the process admitted their involvement. On occasion, the meetings concluded there was no evidence of drug dealing. Decisions were made by a show of hands by attendees. If a meeting decided the evidence was substantial, alleged dealers were warned to cease their activities.

These decisions were taken and implemented by ordinary people many of whom had little previous involvement in community activities. They were implementing a community mandate they believed their neighbours had given. The St Teresa's Gardens Concerned Parents Against Drugs (STG-CPAD) was formed as a result although it continued not to have a structure. Its progress was regularly discussed at Development Committee meetings, led by chairperson Paul Humphrey.

During these, decisions were taken to support the anti-drugs campaigners in several practical ways such as arranging refreshments for those on patrols and by preparing media statements and other published material as required. It was through attending these meetings that I learned about the anti-drug events that were unfolding and also through other conversations separately held with Humphrey and other committee members.

From June 1983 on, the STG-CPAD confronted nine alleged drug dealers at public meetings. The evidence against two was deemed inconclusive and no action was taken. Two others — user-dealers — openly admitted dealing and agreed to stop and did so. Another two in a similar category refused to stop but left the community voluntarily. Three senior dealers were forced to leave having begun dealing again three months after first agreeing to stop.

Their activities became apparent in September 1983 after an incident in which yet another young man was discovered at the back of the flats unconscious from a drugs overdose. Community members resuscitated him and brought him to hospital. They asked who was still selling drugs? Afterwards, the three dealers who had previously agreed to stop were asked to come to the next public meeting.

They denied continued involvement and maintained their stance until confronted by a sister of one who claimed he had sought to involve her and other family members in his drug dealing. The three then acknowledged their continued dealing, but made clear it was their business and they could not be told to stop. The meeting took the view, however, that the three had been given sufficient time over the summer to stop. There was now no alternative for them but to leave the flats. They were given a week to do so.

Next day, two of them sent a solicitor's letter to Paul Humphrey who they identified as one of the STG-CPAD leaders. It stated that legal assistance had been sought to prevent any attempt to have them ejected. As the letter named the two people represented by the solicitor,

The Harm Done

Humphrey copied it and circulated it to each household. He arranged to reconvene the public meeting that evening at which it was decided to evict the three dealers immediately.

The rationale for this decision was that if they were granted a court injunction, they would have police protection. It would then be impossible to have them removed without conflict with the Garda. If the people got them out first, it was believed, neither courts nor Garda could get them back in. Following the meeting, in an action of mass participation, the flats of the three, who had temporarily absented themselves, were stripped of all their furniture. Their belongings were piled up in a bundle in the centre of the square. The mass participation ensured no individual person would be singled out for retaliation.

These evictions represented the most difficult decision for the STG-CPAD. The three people concerned were themselves local, had family ties in the community and had grown up with many of those now responsible for their eviction. They were leading drug dealers in the south city, however, trying to revive their business from within St Teresa's Gardens. Their eviction — the first of its type — was a high point in the STG-CPAD campaign principally because it had so much potential for open conflict, but was achieved without person-to-person violence. This was clearly helped by the fact that the suspected drug dealers had already, prior to the removal of their furniture, left the estate, and revisited later only to remove all their belongings. The action was a stand against those local dealers who continued to sell drugs.

For a three-month period during summer 1983, the STG-CPAD was a source of encouragement to communities in other parts of the city, including the nearby estates of Dolphin House, Fatima Mansions and Bridgefoot Street. Their initial campaign was successful primarily because it was a bottom-up grassroots action and because the drug dealers had yielded to the moral will of an organised community. By September 1983, however, community interests and the drug dealers were at loggerheads. It appeared the group of three were under constant pressure from their gang leader to recommence dealing. Although they were from and lived in the community, they were viewed as acting wilfully against residents' request to cease their trade. Two years previously it had been predicted that the community would lose a confrontation against the dealers if they took a stand. It would probably lead to deeper violence, the previously referred to bloodbath. Indeed, leading up to the three evictions, many in the community believed dealers would use financial resources to mobilise low-level pushers and others to act violently against the STG-CPAD and individual supporters.

Ironically, what convinced them to implement the evictions was the decision of two of the three to threaten court proceedings, thereby seeking outside help. This exposed their vulnerability and their fear of the community's actions. The tactic of people standing together to protect each other seemed to have worked. Previously, drug dealers played on primal fears by threatening violence against them and their families — using the courts would have been unthinkable. By going legal, the dealers inadvertently weakened their own perverse authority giving local people more confidence to act.

Another factor explained the community's new-found confidence. Members of the Dunne family had come under enormous police scrutiny on the back of pressure on the police by Taoiseach Charles Haughey during the Tony Gregory-supported Fianna Fáil Government of 1982.[4] Dunne family members had come before the court, including Larry Dunne. He was convicted of having heroin for supply on June 25, 1983, just six days after the first St Teresa's Gardens public meeting. He was not sentenced until two years later as on the day of his conviction he absconded, having earlier obtained bail to have lunch in a nearby hostelry.[5] A claim of Dunne being discomfited by the CPAD was included in a Sky News TV documentary, Dublin Narcos. The claim was implausible as by then he was already on the run.

Meanwhile, the Garda, using an undercover unit, closed in on other family members including Dunne's brother Michael. He operated from Fatima Mansions and was sentenced in October the same year. In less than twelve months, following protests outside his home on Weaver Square, about 600 metres from St Teresa's Gardens, and following an intervention by the local priest to whom he had offered Christmas food hampers, Boyo Dunne, Larry's brother, voluntarily left the area. He went to Birmingham and, according to local reports, never returned.

STG-CPAD's actions against drug dealing were not always lawful. What they did by evicting people was intrinsically illegal and wrong. From inside the community and by the observations of some of the outsiders involved, however, the evictions were seen as reasonable and justified in the circumstances. Some community members were clearly uneasy with unfolding events, wondering aloud whether it was right to evict neighbours — family members of some — from their own homes. Debates on these matters happened on balconies, stairways, at the local shops and in people's homes. Some made it clear they did not want anything to do with what was evolving.

The Harm Done

The counter arguments were stronger and had widespread support. Heroin use and drug dealing had got to such levels that St Teresa's Gardens residents were overwhelmed. They argued that their community had been under attack, that those perceived as directly responsible — the drug dealers — had shown little restraint in their activities, had deliberately drawn vulnerable young people into their networks, and that the justice and health authorities had shown little capacity to respond or assure the community that a response was imminent. People claimed that outsiders had no right to judge them unless they lived through what St Teresa's Gardens had lived through.

I recall Paul Humphrey at the time claiming that the people had been 'conquered' by the problem, but that their actions against drug dealing brought a form of freedom.[6] The action was for sure cathartic, described by local medical practitioner, Fergus O'Kelly — in an interview with this author — as healing.[7] Immediately after the formation of the STG-CPAD, it would have been difficult to dispute such representations. Having kept their heads down for four years out of fear and denial, people felt they had no option but to fight back. They saw no alternative but direct action, even if this meant acting against people they had grown up with and to whom they were close in other ways like family and friendship.

Minister for Health, Barry Desmond, TD — barely visible — being shown around St Teresa's Gardens, by YDP staff and participants, 1984.
Photo: Derek Speirs ©

Viewing a photo exhibition during Small Club opening, February, 1984.
Photo: Paul Humphrey Collection

CHAPTER 6

A Doomed Youth Project, 1983–5

After a new recruitment process in June 1983, I became the Youth Development Programme's (YDP's) second project leader. By coincidence my appointment started two weeks after the anti-drugs movement was formed, a development that brought new challenges and opportunities for the YDP. By forming a partnership with the Development Committee, the project got off the ground surprisingly quickly in undertaking targeted prevention work. This was partly due to community events described in Chapter 5 that had created a climate of solid neighbourhood support for our activities. There was also a significant openness within the newly established Youth Employment Agency (YEA) to become directly involved in funding the YDP, and in helping to access funds from other state bodies.

The YEA, along with these other bodies, assigned considerable funding directly to the Development Committee to proceed with targeted preventative work, in the form of a Communication Skills Programme. For an initial start-up period, it was agreed I would coordinate this programme under the YDP's auspices. The Development Committee gave the project an under-used section of its community premises, the Small Club. The health board agreed to refurbish it, a temporary measure while progress on a more permanent premises would continue. It is instructive that work to develop this facility never happened.

An important highlight for the YDP was the recruitment of twenty-four young people onto the training / employment scheme, administratively managed by the Development Committee. Most young participants lived in risky situations. Some had previously been involved in heroin use, others in petty crime, some had siblings who used or had used drugs and were considered to be at additional risk as a result.

The Harm Done

As unemployment was visible in the community, the employment of even a small number of young people signalled that things could be different. The YDP gave young people routines, new relationships, an awareness of drug risks and an independent income. They staged open days and other events to showcase their work. On one occasion they attracted considerable media coverage, underlining their progress in contributing to community transformation.[1] In many respects the project reflected the thinking of Terrie Kearney who had advocated for this approach over four years previously, as had her successor Patricia Daly. It underscored that while outside attention on the community focused on heroin users, other young residents had the wherewithal to avoid heroin use or discontinue their involvement. By so doing they had articulated an alternative narrative on young peoples' experiences in socially difficult circumstances.

While the targeted prevention work seemed relatively successful, little progress was made with those whose heroin dependency continued. It had been envisaged that the YDP would recruit two workers to undertake outreach, but previously the health board failed to recruit staff, causing the first project leader to resign. Once again the process was delayed. Substantial differences emerged around the concept of outreach treatment. For some, it involved community-based personnel implementing and monitoring a prescribed, abstinence programme by the National Drug Advisory and Treatment Centre (NDATC) in a community setting. Others like the YDP viewed outreach as engaging with individuals not currently in formal treatment, to build relationships with them over time, helping them to manage their problems without preconditions. This engagement could then be used to build motivation for more formal drug treatment, if desired, through referral, if need be, to the NDATC or similar.

Having undertaken outreach work with local people who used heroin and being familiar with their predicament, I was sceptical that a strengthened NDATC role would make a substantial difference to their drug use. It could potentially work if it radically transformed its suite of interventions and shifted focus away from an institutional to a community base and refrained from always seeking commitments to long-term abstinence. In short, if it introduced methadone maintenance in line with an improved engagement with community-based support personnel, it might be viable.

In the case of St Teresa's Gardens, virtually all those who used heroin had already attended the NDATC, not once but several times. While most had stopped using for varying periods, most had ended up relapsing. Of the very few who had not, it was apparent they had begun to develop serious alcohol problems. The drug-free approach was not working, except perhaps for a tiny few. Whatever way it was viewed, the programme was failing on its own terms and radical alternatives, including methadone maintenance, were needed.

The YDP's alternative outreach approach was influenced by UK developments and by different ideas to those promulgated by abstinence model adherents. Within weeks of starting my new role I organised a study trip to drug outreach, street and other treatment services. These included the Blenheim project in London that facilitated home detoxifications with GP participation[2]; the Kaleidoscope project in Kingston-on-Thames with its strong focus on harm reduction[3] and the Lifeline project in Manchester that combined harm reduction and addiction training for professionals in the field.[4] I met personnel at the shared offices (Hatton Place, London) of Standing Conference on Drug Abuse (SCODA) and Institute for the Study of Drug Dependence (ISDD).[5] Both bodies were strong advocates of alternatives to the abstinence model.

Historically, the UK offered a more tolerant approach to drug problems, albeit one rooted in criminal justice through what was referred to as the British system.[6] Medical doctors could diagnose and prescribe for addiction, provided they kept records. In the late 1960s the system was reformed. The entitlement to prescribe was confined to specified regulated doctors, but was tempered by a greater investment in drugs treatment by developing a small network of drug dependency clinics from which these doctors could operate.[7]

The clinics were multi-disciplinary, led by psychiatrists, and provided psychosocial therapies and opiate substitute treatment (methadone) for detoxification and maintenance purposes. It was significantly different to the US drug free model especially as it acknowledged that many opiate-dependent clients could not or would not become abstinent. The UK approach was at odds with that advocated by Irish health authorities. There was little evidence the latter informed themselves of emerging developments in other countries, such as the UK and elsewhere, other than the US. Although I submitted a detailed report on my study visit to health board management, the ideas garnered were never again referred to in my discussions with them.

While the academic evidence in support of methadone maintenance was available during the 1980s[8] it was not routinely referred to and did not feature in Irish policy discourse. Not that there was any coherent policy discussion at the time — the *First Report of the National Coordinating*

The Harm Done

Committee on Drug Abuse, 1986, did not reference a single international report on drug use. As an aside, it is noteworthy that the contemporary preoccupation with evidence-based policies was not embedded in health policy-making in previous decades. Historically — and often currently in fact — policy-making is not so simple that it follows rational rules in addiction or other fields. Policymakers operate from a multitude of agendas that are framed by different knowledge, political and moral considerations. In this regard, the policy process is not neutral and the influence of vested interests in plans for health reorganisation are often overwhelming.[9]

The NDATC was aghast at the idea of maintenance programmes. In discussions, personnel frequently cited their programme ethos and commitment to achieving a drug-free society in justifying their opposition. In their view it was institutionally prohibited from using intervention formats premised on maintaining a drug addiction unless this was needed for other medical purposes. In a similar vein, Coolmine made clear it would not work at all with people on methadone maintenance, especially as it considered it had a wider advocacy role of opposing alternative harm reduction methods.[10]

The NDATC's stance on methadone use was akin to that of a Catholic hospital which insisted, on moral grounds, that its medical staff should not prescribe the contraceptive pill, unless for purely medical reasons. It meant using methadone only for detoxification or to maintain health stability for pregnant women or for other persons with serious illnesses. While it was understandable that professionals trained in an abstinence model would have difficulty, even problems of conscience, in implementing harm reduction, it did not seem acceptable that a publicly funded national centre should absolutely refuse to implement such strategies.

Similarly, although Coolmine was an independent entity and not subject to statutory directions in its work or programmes, it was nonetheless a major recipient of public funds within the drug treatment space. It seemed incredible that it could absorb such a high level — percentage wise — of the then available resources to operate such a limited, exclusive programme.

The closed-mindedness central to the abstinence approach, however, went much deeper than the scruples of a few front-line professionals or agencies. The previously mentioned unpublished report of the Special Government Task Force on Drug Abuse, 1983 had acknowledged that heroin use was concentrated in socially disadvantaged urban areas rather than randomly distributed throughout Irish society. As a corollary, it had recommended that funding should be targeted at community-based projects in those same areas. The report acknowledged and advocated a grassroots, bottom-up response, whereas the dominant clinical response was top-down.

Based on its attendance figures, the NDATC knew that heroin use was geographically concentrated. But it did not publicly articulate a concern about this neighbourhood aspect. The Government quashed the ministerial conclusions by not publishing the report and by not referring to these recommendations in press statements. It favoured retention of the centralised clinical model of heroin treatment and downgraded the community model before it could even get properly started. In reinforcing the idea of specialised services, it gave the NDATC full control of unreconstructed abstinence treatment.

Because the report was buried, in this pre-social media and pre-Freedom of Information era the public, media and frontline professionals remained unaware for several years of its full details, conclusions and recommendations. Nor did they know the geographical distribution of those who attended programmes at the NDATC. That information was not at the time publicly circulated or made available. The treatment system seemed determined to continue as before, indifferent to and unconcerned by Dublin's main heroin problem being concentrated in a few socially disadvantaged areas. Meanwhile the people most deeply affected by drug use had little prospect of being engaged intensively in treatment through the centralised NDATC abstinence treatment model.

In the wake of Government statements on its unpublished report, health officials weighed in behind the abstinence model. On behalf of the Health Minister, officials met Coolmine, 'to discuss the provision of a suitable therapeutic model for the treatment of drug abusers from socially and educationally deprived backgrounds'.[11] Meanwhile, the health board abandoned the idea of recruiting YDP outreach workers and instead, above the heads of the YDP committee, assigned a counsellor trained in the abstinence model of addiction who was a member of a religious order. This decision was perceived as a major rebuke to the project, its management group, community supporters and to me as project leader and the ideas I had advanced on problem drug-taking since taking up my position.

The newly appointed counsellor, based in the Small Club, operated without any formal relationship with the YDP and had clinical supervision from the NDATC. The counsellor had been recommended to the health board by that centre's clinical director Michael Kelly. Notwithstanding its good intentions, the counselling programme — predicated on unrealistic drug-free aims — never managed to engage substantially with young people with an established record of using heroin, as was the original intention.

Meanwhile, the health board adopted an abrasive, confrontational attitude in its dealings with the local Development Committee that had control over the Small Club community premises. Having aided its refurbishment, they assumed they were entitled to take full control of the centre's use and management. At one stage it was proposed that all those attending the centre and staff be subjected to urine testing for drugs. This matter was very contentious. While some community members supported it, the Development Committee and the YDP were set against it. The committee, which had a Dublin Corporation licence to manage the centre, rejected the proposal and rebutted the health board's efforts to take over the premises, warning them off from further interference.

On another occasion, health board management sought to gain control over the prevention resources made available to the Development Committee through third-party state bodies, principally the YEA. Later I was reprimanded for what was seen as my failure to help the health board achieve the desired transfer. At the time, health board executives had set up a separate, independent training agency with its own senior staff acting in charge, later serving on the company's board of directors, post-incorporation. Health board management wanted the funding redirected to this training agency rather than the Development Committee, thus giving them, not the latter, control of the assigned resources.

Eventually the health board programme manager informed the director of community care in a letter copied to me that a report on my performance had been received and reviewed. While acknowledging the success of the work being undertaken, the letter warned of a commonly held view within senior management that I saw my loyalty as 'being to organisations other than the Board, and that this has created hostility which has not helped working relationships'. I was expected to give the board my 'absolute loyalty', it was stated.

The missive was provocative and consistent with an institutional mindset seeking scapegoats for its own failings. Despite asking, I never saw the report referred to and was never told what organisations were meant by 'other'. But it seemed evident, and not for the first time — given its previous response to Terrie Kearney's work — that health board management saw the Development Committee as a hostile organisation.

A Doomed Youth Project, 1983–5

They considered it remiss of me not to facilitate a transfer of resources to the health board's own training agency. Having already lost one project leader, they seemed determined to lose a second. It was clear the partnership model in which different agencies came together to mitigate locally the problems confronting young people was imperilled, mainly by the actions of its primary sponsor. Loathed by health management, the YDP for as long as it had a grassroots ethos, had little prospect of ongoing stability. With other more contentious factors also influencing the overall attitude and approach of the health authorities, the project was indeed doomed.

On April 23, 1984, a few weeks after a series of incidents involving a shooting, and two kidnappings that were later followed by arrests and convictions of members of an armed gang (see Chapter 7), I was visited at home by two members of the Garda Special Branch, which was responsible for investigating threats to state security and the monitoring of persons and organisations considered to pose a threat to state security. They questioned me about my work, and asked: 'Do you know the type of people you are associating with in St Teresa's Gardens?' I was taken aback both by the visit and question, but I responded that I could not discuss work matters without my employer's explicit permission.

After a short stand-off at my front door, they left. I later told the director of community care of the visit and being asked about my work. He informed me — in a manner that suggested he was offering a reasonable explanation — that health board management was under considerable political pressure. This was so because the YDP and the Development Committee were perceived as too close to the anti-drugs movement. Tellingly, he failed to express concern, as I had expected, about their reference to 'the type of people' I was associating with.

He made clear his disapproval of comments I had made at a public event, and he claimed that in the presence of several senior health figures, politicians and senior gardaí, I had criticised the health minister, Barry Desmond TD, who was also present, and that this was unacceptable. The Development Committee had asked me to make an opening address at the event — the formal opening of the Small Club premises after its refurbishment — and indeed in advance of the meeting I consulted the Director about what I should say. As it happened, I did not criticise the minister at all, but during the event I did make an impromptu, well-received comment about some media coverage of the anti-drug activists. However, on behalf of the Development Committee, Paul Humphrey in his brief statement, at the same event, having brought the minister on an

The Harm Done

estate walkabout, addressed him directly, stating it was time he and his Department got their act together to provide proper funding to local drug projects.

This criticism was not new, but a repeat of comments made by Humphrey a few weeks earlier in the minister's presence at a public meeting hosted by the Labour Party. The minister knew about this criticism before agreeing to attend the Small Club opening. Besides, as a seasoned politician he could be expected to take that particular criticism on the chin. The problem was more that health board management felt criticised. As previously executive management had dumped this criticism onto the director, he in turn felt compelled to dump it on someone else. And as before following the Dublin City Council meeting in October 1981, I was the convenient scapegoat.

I was obviously concerned by his comments. The idea that I should be required to accept responsibility for Humphrey's reasoned comments and opinions was bad enough, but the perception that the YDP was too close to anti-drug campaigners was disingenuous. Health management had made no progress in securing an alternative premises for the YDP and as a result it had to share the Small Club with other groups. The YDP had no direct involvement with the STG-CPAD, although I and other staff participated in a CPAD protest march about the Government's lack of action on the issue in February 1984 (see Chapter 7). The anti-drugs campaign could not be ignored by anybody working in the community whether or not they had a base there. There were several ongoing friendly exchanges between activists and YDP staff, as there were with personnel from other projects and services in the wider area. This included the social work service, community welfare and housing welfare, and education services.

My exchange with the director signalled a gathering opposition to the YDP. I believe this arose not because of any perceived association it had with CPAD, but because its work did not fit the then centralised punitive narrative on drugs and drug users. As already mentioned, the Department of Health and the health board had opened up discussions with Coolmine on developing an alternative youth treatment programme for socially disadvantaged youth. Funding for this initiative, which never got off the ground in the manner expected, was announced later that same year.[12] Coolmine's main programme, based on a 'tough love' ideology, did not resonate with young people. Its sponsoring of the value-laden Federation of Parents for Drug Free Youth (renamed National Federation of Community Action on Drugs), and its slogan Only Natural Highs for

A Doomed Youth Project, 1983–5

Our Kids was a definitive statement about its bizarre understanding of young people's needs and aspirations.[13]

Coolmine's staff were mainly former residents — or graduates — with little evidence of formal training in working with young people. It was reported in 1982 that young offenders, given a choice, would opt for a prison regime rather than Coolmine out of concern for its 'strict and bizarre discipline' and that it 'often involved personal humiliation for the addicts'.[14] Given its uncompromising ideological ethos, it appeared that Coolmine lacked capacity to modify what was then a highly questionable therapeutic model, for which it presented no evidential support, into a youth intervention programme, for which less ideology and more programme flexibility would be required.

That the health board was retreating from a youth outreach programme in a community long-regarded as disproportionately affected by heroin in favour of Coolmine was a monumental affront to the intelligence of frontline workers. They, myself included, had made such huge commitments against the odds to getting the YDP established. Furthermore, it was a snub to community members, young people and their parents, who had taken substantial risks in creating favourable environmental conditions for the project to operate. It was hypocritical that while the minister and his officials were shown around St Teresa's Gardens by young people on the YDP discussions were already in place to supplant the project with a Coolmine controlled alternative.

The developments were consistent with Government's refusal to acknowledge where drug problems were concentrated, and their association with socio-economic disadvantage. Instead, they preferred the idea as expressed at the time by then Junior Minister in the Department of Justice, Nuala Fennell (1935–2009). In the Dáil, she stated that the 'sons and daughters of judges or bank managers' were as likely to be 'drug addicts' as people from 'any of the more publicised areas'.[15] While Fennell had a valid point on the general distribution of society's drug use (including cocaine and cannabis use), it seemed inappropriate for her to say this in the context of a drugs debate driven primarily by the heroin problem, which was demonstrably concentrated in specific areas. As a member of the *Special Government Task Force on Drug Abuse,* Fennell would have known about this concentration. Although Coolmine had an independent mindset, particularly on its treatment model, it would reliably maintain the contentious political line that the drug problem was classless.

In 1985, two years into my role as YDP project leader, my relationship

The Harm Done

with health board management had deteriorated to the point where my position was untenable. My work was micro-managed by central executives making it increasingly difficult to undertake basic development activities or to draw down agreed funds. And as previously mentioned management had resiled from appointing two outreach treatment workers. Operational decisions were taken over my head.

I was bizarrely threatened with disciplinary proceedings following a relatively benign, spontaneously-arranged morning radio interview. Paradoxically it was viewed by several health board personnel as positive towards the health authorities since they were identified as funding the YDP. I came to realise that health board management, at the time and for a long period afterward, had no official media strategy or spokesperson and lacked an ability to understand public communications. They were blinded by the need to control their own frontline messengers. The problem was not the message, but the wrong messenger. It was one of three separate threats to take disciplinary action. The underlying problem was trust and it was obvious that no matter how the YDP progressed, the threats would continue. I was seen as disloyal. It was difficult for me to discuss this conflict with managers who believed that the more power they conceded to the local community, the less power they themselves had.

I eventually resigned and took up a new external work opportunity. Health board management wound down the YDP. Although it assigned a third project leader, in a relatively short period it withdrew staff to a central base. YDP activities continued to operate through other funding. But without a coherent health-based structure, this too gradually disappeared. Other state agencies pulled back from direct engagement other than to supply already committed funding.

I had worked in the south inner city for five years: a year as a community social worker, two years as community worker and a further two years as project leader. The common thread was to develop and implement strategies from a community development perspective: outreach, engagement with local leaders, identification and quantification of needs and issues, training, project development, resource negotiation and management.

As stated in this book's introduction, my involvement with drug issues was accidental, but what came after was not. From the outset, I informed myself of relevant literature and policies as outlined in previous chapters. I read virtually back-to-back the Consumer Union editors 1972 report *Licit and Illicit Drugs*[16], which remains today, over fifty years after

A Doomed Youth Project, 1983–5

it was published, a comprehensive compendium of issues concerning drug dependence, prevention and treatment. While the book is highly readable, it does not over-simplify. Foremost in its pragmatic conclusions is that many problems associated with illicit drug use could be overcome if they were more readily available.

The Consumer Union editors were particularly supportive of methadone maintenance treatments. I picked up the book on a visit to the US in May 1983 just before starting as YDP project leader. Between the knowledge derived from analysing its contents and other material from the aforementioned UK visit, I was determined to utilise pragmatism in the YDP's development. To little avail. The YDP had notable successes in showing how targeted prevention could succeed in diverting young people from problematic drug use. But the situation of those already deeply entrenched seemed beyond resolution. While nobody believed methadone was a remedy, and its introduction since has proven deeply challenging for providers and their clients, it at least offered the possibility that people's situations could be stabilised. With stability, more and more could be drawn into treatment and health monitoring and lives could be saved.

For those early heroin users in the late 1970s and early 1980s, years of untreated addiction lay ahead. Meanwhile, their parents were often left caring for adult children with appalling illnesses. Various community-based health and social service personnel felt they were operating in a straightjacket given the options for responding to these problems and their ramifications. Taking together the physical and mental health of people who used heroin, child protection issues, and responsibilities for new care arrangements to support increasing numbers of grandparents rearing their grandchildren due to bereavement, illness or other parental absences, were overwhelming.

By the late 1990s, twenty-three (37%) of the sixty-three persons identified in the 1981 research exercise in St Teresa's Gardens (see Chapter 3) had died prematurely. Of the forty still alive then, twenty-seven have since died, the 27th died in September 2023, just weeks before this book was completed. In total, fifty individuals, or 79% of the entire group, have died. Undoubtedly some deaths were from natural causes or serious illnesses, but most were premature, avoidable and associated with their drug use. It had disastrous impacts on their families and friends. This heroin ordeal was replicated elsewhere in Dublin's inner city and suburban working-class areas. It leaves an unprecedented level of harm done, individual and family trauma, and community disorganisation, greater than the

The Harm Done

totality of other localised events in the state's history. But there has been no redress, no detailed examination, no proper accountability, and little reference to it, let alone analysis, in official contemporary discussions about Dublin's drug history.

Parents and children gather for community festival, June 1984.
Photo: Paul Humphrey Collection

A banner carried by young people from St Teresa's Gardens in a protest march to Government Buildings February 29, 1984.
Photo: Derek Speirs ©

CHAPTER 7

Community and Political Conflict

During the period 1983–85 (see Chapter 5), direct action against drug dealing by residents in inner-city estates was widely perceived as successful in offering respite to communities whose members felt abandoned by mainstream bodies. The Youth Development Programme felt their impact and most young people spoke about the anti-drug activities in positive terms. Some gave out about the 'vigis' as they called them however, mainly because their nightly presence on the estate could indirectly affect other social activities. In October 1983, young people got involved in helping the STG-CPAD prepare a Halloween victory dance. The following June 1984, they organised a community festival in Player Wills playing fields, behind the flats, which was opened by musicians including Donal Lunny and Davy Spillane. For the festival they also organised an afternoon fancy-dress party for children. The atmosphere on both occasions was fun, colourful and festive.

In parallel, outside inner city estates, a wider negative attitude to anti-drugs activists began to emerge, especially after some Sinn Féin / IRA members threw their weight behind the movement, at a time when they were under considerable political pressure arising from the killing of a Garda recruit and an army soldier during an IRA shootout (see below). Although the media focus in relation to the CPAD was on Sinn Féin's involvement, they were not alone politically in expressing an interest. Members of the Labour Party's Militant Tendency supported the anti-drugs campaign. Labour Youth showed an interest and through this involvement recruited local young people from St Teresa's Gardens into its social and political activities. At one stage Labour Youth advocated that trade unions get behind the anti-drugs movement.[1]

The Inchicore branch of the Democratic Socialist Party (DSP) that merged with Labour a few years later was involved in giving leadership to the anti-drugs campaign in St Michael's Estate. This was mainly through the involvement of teacher Michael Conaghan who was based in the Inchicore Vocational School. In 2011 he was elected as a Labour Party TD for a single term in the Dublin South Central constituency.

In general, other political representatives refrained from publicly expressing solidarity with the residents' actions. The Labour Party Deputy Leader, and Minister for Health, Barry Desmond was, from an early stage, viewed as particularly antagonistic and in December 1983, six months after the STG-CPAD commenced their anti-drugs actions, in the Dáil he warned residents' associations, not to 'succumb to the deliberate manipulation of the problem' by the 'Provisional IRA'.[2]

When asked by north inner city Independent TD Tony Gregory to fund such groups, Desmond replied that local responses needed to be guided directly by the health authorities and their personnel in the field. It was perceived as a hurtful comment towards leaders in several inner city communities. Gregory was clearly annoyed. It was widely known by then that the health board was stifling rather than supporting community initiatives. In the Dáil it was claimed, for example, that health officials had undermined the work of the Ballymun Youth Action Project set up a few years earlier to address drug problems.[3] Meanwhile, amid these criticisms Government was channelling funds to the Coolmine-supported National Federation Community Action on Drugs[4] — it had no foothold in any of the communities most affected by heroin and it was generally perceived as a middle-class body upholding the contention that drug use arose from individual pathology. Yet it was being promised more funding for additional activities.[5]

When the anti-drugs group in St Teresa's Gardens was started in 1983 no political party, Sinn Féin included, appeared to have any members living in the area or was involved in local actions. During the general election in November 1982, residents organised a town hall election hustings. Only two politicians turned up: Eric Byrne then of the Workers' Party; and Ben Briscoe (1934–2023) of Fianna Fáil. In response to criticism of political representatives, Briscoe said that in general there was a poor turn-out in elections from voters in the flat complexes and that politicians, himself included, lacked motivation to canvas in these places. Briscoe had a reputation for startling honesty and had once openly criticised his party's leader, Charles Haughey, and what he referred to as his cult of personality. People at the hustings were taken aback by his comments and criticised him. But at least he showed up. Sinn Féin's absence was hardly surprising as they had no election candidate or political profile. Which wasn't the case for Fine Gael or the Labour Party.

Apart from Christy Burke in the north inner city— who stood in the February 1982 general election but not in the November election the same year — Sinn Féin had little political presence in Dublin. It did not run other candidates in Dáil elections in the city until 1987 when it unsuccessfully contested eight of the city's eleven constituencies. The 1987 elections followed the H-Block political status hunger strike campaign of 1981, which led to the deaths of Bobby Sands MP (1954–81). On June 11 in a Dáil election during the hunger strikes, one participant Kieran Doherty (1955–81) and a H-Block prisoner (not on hunger strike) Paddy Agnew were both elected for the border constituencies of Sligo / Leitrim and Louth. Doherty died a few weeks after being elected. The deaths of hunger strikers during May–August 1981 had a profound emotional impact on society. Some young people from working class backgrounds, in particular, got involved with Sinn Féin as a result.

Following the hunger strike mobilisation, Sinn Féin, adopted a two-pronged approach of political and community activism, on the one hand, and continued support for armed combat, on the other, the so called 'armalite and ballot-box' strategy.[6] In 1986, Sinn Féin abandoned Dáil abstentionism making way for a stronger engagement in politics and the election of its first TD in 1997,[7] although it was 2002, before the engagement in politics translated into multiple Dáil seats (5). While it lost a seat in 2007, the performance since has been impressive: 2011 (14), 2016 (23), and 2020 (37). It is reasonably expected that following the next general election — due early 2025 at the latest — that the party will increase its seats further and most likely will lead government.

Undoubtedly the anti-drug movements gave Sinn Féin a tremendous opportunity to initiate their grassroots political campaign in working class communities as they had already done in Northern Ireland. The idea that they were manipulating community leaders in St Teresa's Gardens was completely off the mark, although the same could not be said for the CPAD Central Committee, which was established in 1984 mainly at the instigation of Sinn Féin activists. In the north inner city by-election in November 1983, Christy Burke canvassed on the back of his anti-drugs work and long-term involvement in the local community. He more than doubled his share of the vote from three percentage points in February 1982's general election to seven in the by-election. The result alone was not that significant, but it indicated the possibility of a rising trend for Sinn Féin activism in poor communities. Two years later he was the first (provisional) Sinn Féin candidate to be elected to Dublin City Council.

A significant intervention in the developing story of Sinn Féin's supposed CPAD infiltration was a report from RTÉ's flagship current affairs programme Today Tonight in December 1983 a few weeks after the by-election. It highlighted Burke's involvement in the action against drug dealers in Hardwicke Street as signifying possible IRA engagement. It was often claimed at the time that some programming output was over-influenced by an anti-Sinn Féin faction of Workers' Party supporters in the state broadcaster.[8]

While Sinn Féin involvement in CPAD was undoubtedly gathering momentum, it was perfectly legitimate for members of a registered political party — as distinct from the banned IRA — to become involved in community affairs. After all, Christy Burke was already involved in community matters before becoming involved with the drugs issue. It seemed the RTE report was encouraging people to infer that those with links to protest groups Sinn Féin was involved with were naive in not recognising that they were a front for IRA violence.

In St Teresa's Gardens there was antipathy towards the TV programme makers. Although two years later a different Today Tonight programme team, led by award-winning journalist Mary Raftery (1957–2012), adopted a more sympathetic conciliatory approach in its coverage of community events, the December 1983 report came to symbolise the community's isolation from the establishment whose view seemed to contend that anti-drugs community groups were superficially dealing with the problem and being manipulated.

A main effect of the manipulation allegation was that it attributed achievements gained by grassroots anti-drugs actions to the party when it was not initially involved — apart from Burke. The local political benefits of such an association were obviously not lost on individual Sinn Féin members who wasted little time in demonstrating their 'credentials' were well earned. In Tallaght, for example, ex-IRA man, John Noonan took the lead in forming a CPAD group. The wider aim was to build a community-based political movement around the drugs issue. Previously Noonan had been involved with the unemployment issue locally, but it gained no traction. With the drugs issue Sinn Féin members could potentially, draw a clear distinction between their organisational tactics and those of other parties.

Initially, it was claimed that political differences centred on Sinn Féin's willingness to support CPAD as a working class struggle. Other political parties did not, it was stated. As already mentioned however, Sinn Féin activists were not alone in providing this support. A key moment for the party in establishing the essential difference between it and others occurred after an incident in 1984 when an anti-drugs campaigner was shot and wounded as he spoke to a neighbour in St Teresa's Gardens.[9] The incident was interpreted as a retaliation by drug dealers and other criminals against the local community. STG-CPAD activists apportioned some blame to the media which they claimed, had used a vigilante narrative for describing the community's actions.[10] The incident, coupled with a protest march past the estate's entrance by the self-styled Concerned Criminals Action Committee (CCAC)[11] — led by Martin Cahill — greatly heightened community tensions and concerns that they would lack protection from further reprisals.

On March 11, 1984, a few weeks after the February shooting, the first of two kidnappings of members of Cahill's criminal gang took place. An undercover Garda operation foiled the second kidnapping. Both men were released and a group of men were arrested, charged and later convicted of the abductions.[12] In the aftermath of the arrests when the matter remained sub judice local speculation was ongoing about whether the IRA were involved in the kidnappings: were they an IRA retaliation against the February shooting or because the IRA had escalated its own conflicts with Cahill? Whatever happened, there had been no public call or discussion about retaliations by the local community.

Fear was growing in St Teresa's Gardens that its reputation as the 'people who took on the pushers'[13] could end up costing residents dearly. Many were especially wary of getting caught up in crossfire between established criminals such as Cahill and the IRA. The shooting added momentum to staging a well-attended citywide CPAD march to protest against Government inaction and it attracted a favourable *Irish Times* editorial.[14] However, a divide emerged among residents on the future conduct of their anti-drugs activities.

On one side were those who proposed that their anti-drug actions should be confined to their own area only. Since this was considered successful, all that was required was for people to remain vigilant through regular evening walking patrols and information meetings. On the other side were those who believed they should get behind a newly formed Central Committee of CPAD groups and be available to support anti-drug actions elsewhere. Initially, the Central Committee focus was to share information between different groups. But it later developed into the main instigator for several targeted actions against alleged drug dealers and others throughout Dublin. Thus, members of the Central Committee gathered and processed their own intelligence on alleged drug dealing and these were presented at meetings held in the communities in which the alleged dealers lived.[15]

Paul Humphrey from the local Development Committee was the leading proponent of the former view of pausing an involvement with the Central Committee. He and I shared an office in the Small Club so we constantly related our work to each other in general terms. He had an organisational involvement with the STG-CPAD: planning and convening meetings, preparing refreshments for people on patrols and played a role in dealing with media queries. Several times, he was interviewed by journalists about anti-drug activities in St Teresa's Gardens. During 1983–84 he had become their unofficial spokesperson, the public face of their local campaign.

We often discussed media matters generally, and also the various offers he had to do interviews. He was circumspect about the media, however, and by instinct he was disinclined to trust their attitude towards inner city areas. In most instances he preferred to avoid contact, or comment, if he could, but given that media was going to cover events in any case, he did his best to keep them updated. He regularly challenged journalists around allegations that the IRA was in control of events, underlining that while they might be involved elsewhere, they were not involved in St Teresa's Gardens. Indeed he challenged politicians, both in public and in person, on this matter also.

During a Labour Party conference on the drugs issue held in the Gresham Hotel on February 5th, 1984, he criticised the Health Minister, Barry Desmond TD, among others, who had 'suggested that community action against drugs campaigns are sinister, because they have the support of paramilitary organisations'. He insisted that actions in St Teresa's Gardens were taken by 'the people' and 'by them solely'. The 'support of other people' was welcomed, he said, 'so long as they were prepared to follow the decisions and actions of the people'. He insisted that the campaign 'never had any involvement with a paramilitary campaign'.[16]

After the first of the aforementioned kidnappings Humphrey was arrested for questioning as was John Noonan.[17] Both were released within a few hours. Humphrey was deeply annoyed that the gardaí had arrested him, although at the same time as the second kidnapping more local people were arrested for questioning and later released, and never charged. Humphrey lived in St Teresa's Gardens and was involved in community activities for several years, an involvement that brought him into direct contact with several politicians, with whom he generally had good relationships.

In the previous year Humphrey had taken up a post as community worker with funding from the Inner City Inter-Departmental Committee. His role made him aware that while the STG-CPAD actions were having a positive impact locally, the community needed to move on and get behind other issues. He was especially involved in supporting the rehousing of new tenants into vacant flats and had a role in supporting the Youth Development Programme (YDP) (Chapter 6). Humphrey's community leadership was important for the YDP. He was effective in garnering community support for the project and challenging those community members who criticised it or argued that certain young people should be excluded.

Humphrey knew that habitual heroin users needed access to treatment. There was an urgency in mobilising community efforts to support its provision. He was concerned that too long a focus on marching against drug dealers would not only detract from the needs of this drug-using group who were at risk of being scapegoated, but that the whole community would be tarnished — as he was through his arrest — with other anti-drug activities outside of their control.

Both approaches to anti-drug activities in St Teresa's Gardens were supported in different ways. Most residents would have felt relief about bringing anti-drug actions to a conclusion, thereby removing the pressure they felt under to be involved in protests while relatively secure in the view that the worst — in terms of open drug-dealing — was over. The tangible threat that had created so much fear had passed. People were anxious to find normality. Some got involved, along with Humphrey, in other community activities. A significant number remained loyal to the Central Committee approach and continued to participate in marches in other areas.

The tensions between both sets of advocates came to a head in the June 1984 European election in the Dublin constituency. It was contested for Sinn Féin by John Noonan, who as well as being a former IRA member was also a member of the Central Committee. A committee member asked Humphrey to close-off the Small Club building for a day to coincide with a canvass by Sinn Féin leader Gerry Adams shortly after he had recovered from a UDA assassination attempt.

The request was to allow a meeting in the building between Central Committee members and Adams. The intended PR exercise anticipated a small press entourage with their leader, but it was also considered a

The Harm Done

gesture of thanks to Sinn Féin members for their anti-drug action support. As manager of the Small Club, Humphrey refused permission to use the building while services were in progress.

Relations between the Central Committee, on the one side, and Humphrey and his employer, the local Development Committee, on the other, were inevitably strained. Humphrey's decision had particular importance for the YDP. Had the centre closed and the project ceased for a day, it would have had several negative consequences, as it was already on tenterhooks with health officials on other matters (see Chapter 6).

A few months later a Central Committee decision that they should not on principle cooperate with gardaí, also raised concerns, especially as there was little cause to have such contact, in any case. The decision's underlying rationale, centred around the series of arrests at the time of the kidnappings. On this basis it was suggested that gardaí were harassing anti-drugs activists. For some activists the gardaí were thus perceived as an enemy in the committee's actions against drug dealers. Several residents had misgivings about the gardaí, for sure, and were also critical about their lack of readiness in responding to drug problems. It was far-fetched however to cast them as an enemy, and all that might entail, particularly given the Northern Ireland Troubles, and the tensions there, not only around policing, but that both the Royal Ulster Constabulary (RUC) and the IRA were engaged in violent conflict.

At the time Sinn Féin denied that the IRA was involved directly with the Central Committee.[18] The committee's decision however reflected Sinn Féin's then position of non-cooperation with the state's police and security services. There was an ongoing risk that non-cooperation could lead to confrontation. During the troubles, IRA members were prohibited, by internal rules, from taking 'armed action' against either the army or gardaí.[19] The rules on defensive action were less certain, especially as the IRA, down south, engaged in multiple armed robberies and other activities, to raise funds for their military campaign.[20]

In December 1983, as previously mentioned, a Garda recruit and an army private were fatally wounded during a shootout involving IRA members and security forces in the rescue of kidnapped supermarket executive Don Tidey.[21] The gang escaped. The incident caused widespread outrage. In its aftermath, when pressed on whether it indicated a change in IRA policy towards Irish security personnel, Sinn Féin president, Gerry Adams clarified that it did not and stated: 'I think that it (the two deaths) is regrettable and that, I must point this out, is no reflection on the IRA volunteers that were involved, because they were in a position where they were doing their duty'.[22] Unsurprisingly, the incident, and Adams's comment, generated considerable political and media comment and led to calls, not acted upon, that the party be proscribed.

The following August, a few months after the Central Committee's 1984 decision not to cooperate with the gardaí, a group of men mounted an attack on a post office cash delivery, firing at a Garda escort at Drumree, Co Meath. Garda Frank Hand, was killed. Three men were sentenced to life imprisonment for Hand's capital murder. The attack had the hallmarks of an IRA action although this was denied at the time.[23] By then, following public outrage in the aftermath of the Tidey kidnapping, the IRA appeared to talk down their involvement in this type of militant action in the south. The tactic was repeated in the wake of a foiled attempted bank robbery in Enniscorthy, Co Wexford, a few years later in 1990, following which six people — including former Central Committee PRO, Brian Kenna — were convicted and sentenced.[24] Those involved in both Enniscorthy and Drumree incidents were later released under the Good Friday Agreement confirming were it needed that the incidents were indeed IRA actions.[25]

The Central Committee's attitude towards the gardaí underlined that it, as distinct from individual CPAD groups, had by summer 1984 — twelve months after the CPAD group in St Teresa's Gardens formed — adopted an ambivalent attitude towards policing. By then members of Sinn Féin regularly emphasised that its party rather than others were front and centre in supporting anti-drug activities. However, even though individuals from other parties were involved in local CPAD groups, and while a few expressed concern about Garda inactivity on drug issues, there was little prospect they would equivocate on the overall role of the gardaí. Apart from Sinn Féin, which supported the IRA's armed campaign, it was simply impossible for others to support people for 'doing their duty' if that led to the reasonable interpretation that use of violence was also supported. Following the 1984 decision to withdraw cooperation from the gardaí, the one Democratic Socialist Party branch associated with the Central Committee withdrew from further involvement.

It was to the credit of people in St Teresa's Gardens and other estates that when it really mattered, during 1983-84, their initial actions against drug dealers were not tainted by paramilitary influences. The self-serving and opportunistic engagement by paramilitaries in retaliatory actions changed matters, for sure, and in the public eye it succeeded in discrediting the people's achievements, even though the people had no hand, act or part in the kidnappings. The blemish would remain and paradoxically it added legitimacy to Garda criticisms of anti-drug activists.

The kidnappings were even more reprehensible given that Paul Humphrey — who was identified as a community spokesperson — had vehemently and openly challenged media and political commentators about paramilitary infiltration. His stance on this matter was well known. Following the kidnappings his position became more difficult to defend however, both externally to media and other outside bodies and internally within St Teresa's Gardens. He ceased a direct involvement with the CPAD and concentrated more on the Development Committee and on the YDP. He also mobilised care and income support to individuals and their families who were impacted because of drug-related illnesses and later HIV / AIDS. He was particularly proud of this work especially given that — during the late 1980s — few others were prepared to do so.

At their outset local CPAD groups had been autonomous entities, formed to mobilise peacefully against drug dealing in their own communities. They lacked formal structures and had no formally elected leaders. They nonetheless managed to forge and maintain a practice of open participation and democratic decision-making with the sole and exclusive focus of bringing an end to heroin dealing in their areas. It is particularly unfortunate that at an early stage when groups like the STG-CPAD formed they were not, as requested by Tony Gregory among others, given the institutional and wider political encouragement, however nuanced, that they deserved. Instead, they were criticised and undermined for standing up to a problem they had lived with for so long. Without institutional supports for their work — such as were given to the National Federation of Community Action on Drugs — it was inevitable, as predicted by the previously referenced March 1, 1984 *Irish Times* editorial, that others would take advantage, and seek to control it for political or other purposes.

Meanwhile in the background, following the demise of Dunne gang members, other more ruthless and violent criminals were already getting involved in drug-dealing. The pressures on community groups to sustain local anti-drugs campaigns mounted, thereby leaving them open to further exploitation.

A second wave of heroin use during the early 1990s created the basis for new anti-drugs community movements across the city. At first, some renewed the tactics of CPAD's Central Committee. Others such as Community Response and Citywide had a broader concern and were more focused on bringing a collection of bodies together around a wider range of drug-related issues and strategies (see Chapter 8) in a manner that drew a clear line between, on the one side, community mobilisation and peaceful protests, and on the other, violent anti-drug actions.

The CPAD movement, initiated in Hardwicke Street, but strengthened through the activities in St Teresa's Gardens, had a hugely important effect on community attitudes towards local drug problems and on local people's potential to assume control over related problems. The phrase 'the protection of the people' exemplified the moral authority of a mobilised collective, standing together in peaceful solidarity and, although their intentions were tainted by external developments, the movement was a defining chapter in the history of Dublin's drug problems and, more than anything else that had been done previously, it established that community engagement needed to be central to developing and leading a local response.

Barry Cullen (Director, ALDP), Joe O'Rourke (ALDP Board Chairman) and Chris Flood, TD (Junior Minister for Drugs) at launch of ALDP Annual Report, 1990.
Photo: Tommy Clancy ©

'Hand of Hope' sculpture by Leonardo Benasalvas, Donore Avenue, erected by the community of St Teresa's Gardens, 2007, in memory of all who passed away through addiction
Photo: Aindriú Ó Conaill

CHAPTER 8

Community Model for Managing Drug Problems

I joined the Ana Liffey Drug Project, a national addiction service based in Dublin, as director in 1989. I had been out of direct work on drugs for three years. During that time, I had done work on a project about community and the media[1], and also a research project on policy issues arising from the work of the Second EC Poverty Programme to Combat Poverty (1985–89).[2] My intention was to do further work on community development, but when the Ana Liffey position came up, I applied. This was mainly because I had so much unfinished business with drug issues after working in the south inner city and also in 1988 I had written an article in the *Irish Times* about the need for alternative drug treatments arising from the AIDS problem.[3]

My specific interest in the project arose from the few times I had called into its Abbey Street centre Dublin on behalf of a young man I was in touch with. He had serious health issues due to drugs and I was in personal contact with his family. The project's pragmatic, non-judgmental approach impressed me. Although its funding position was precarious I was interested in the challenge of helping to secure statutory funding to support its unique approach.

Within a short time, I met several people in Ana Liffey from the south inner city who had started using heroin during the late 1970s. I knew them from my work in St Teresa's Gardens. Many had contracted HIV and AIDS, a development that led to their alienation, stigmatisation and abandonment. I met young people from other estates also — including Ballyfermot, Clondalkin and Tallaght — who were part of second heroin use wave and had similar struggles with drug-related health and social problems. They tried desperately to access methadone treatment and other facilities. Many of the original south inner city group were trying to avert an early death. They were dealing with the stress of managing serious illness or rearing teenage children who themselves were highly vulnerable to problem drugs and the lifestyle and stigma that went with that.

The Ana Liffey Drug Project was founded in 1982 by Jesuit priest, Frank Brady, along with his friend and colleague, Mara de Lacy. Brady lived and worked in the north inner city. The pair set about forming a low threshold service to reach out to people who used heroin with no preconditions of abstinence. Where possible, the service supported clients who wished to become drug free. But in most instances the service's aim was to help continuous users and do so in a way that reduced a variety of drug-related harms. The absence of preconditions established the project's credentials as the first drug service in Ireland to operate from a harm-reduction ethos. Brady and de Lacy opened in a Dublin city centre premises on Abbey Street and operated an eclectic mix of health and social care interventions. They relied on friendly contacts in the business world to fund activities. Its ethos was similar to that in Kaleidoscope, London (see Chapter 6), although initially a lot less organised.

The low threshold approach was then considered unorthodox, an affront even to the then dominant abstinence treatment mindset that excluded those not yet ready to make a long-term commitment to life without drugs. The project was considered soft on illicit drug control. In its early years it had no health funding. It did succeed, however, with support from then Labour Minister and future Taoiseach Bertie Ahern in whose constituency the project was based, in placing its semi-voluntary staff on a labour employment scheme.

This first staff group consisted mainly of recently qualified professionals. Instead of taking up permanent positions in statutory bodies they opted to spend a few years in the state's only agency openly committed to an alternative model. Some were trained in social work and advocated a community development approach. Open engagement with service users to help develop their participation in project development was considered important. When I joined in 1989, staff were all full-time employees — but funding remained precarious.

As has been stated, (see Chapter 4) the main drug treatment services in Ireland at the time had accepted as self-evident that interventions should aim to get clients drug free and keep them that way. An understandable ideal, but Ana Liffey's view was that no treatment technologies were capable of achieving this. Drug addicts could, and frequently were, detoxified and helped to become drug free. More often than not, though, they were using again relatively soon after finishing treatment. At the time, in the late 1980s, we were aware of a drugs policy re-think in Scotland[4] and in Merseyside[5] arising from concerns about intravenous drug use and HIV, and also that the 1988 report on *AIDS and Drugs Misuse* by the UK's Advisory Council on the Misuse of Drugs, supported new ways of working with drug users.[6] Furthermore, the newly established (1989) Merchant's Quay Drug Project (now Merchant's Quay Ireland) advocated a strong harm reduction model that provided 'advice on cleaning needles, safer injecting and safer sex'.[7]

We believed that we and Merchants Quay were ahead of the curve in advocating this alternative approach, one later emulated in a network of community-based treatment centres set up during the mid- to late-1990s. Mainstream drug services, for their part, and to the detriment of those seriously dependent on heroin and other opiates, lagged seriously behind. In many respects they failed to see that the abstinence model they so strongly advocated was not only highly contested by the evidence, but stored up serious private and public health consequences.[8]

In my time in the Ana Liffey we put a lot of effort into trying to conceive and explain the alternative model. We invited into our regular discussions external personnel from primary care health and social services to help us tease out how an alternative might operate. While the concept of harm reduction was understood as describing this alternative, we preferred to conceptualise it as a 'community' model. For this, we drew on the 1982 report on *Treatment and Rehabilitation* by the UK's Advisory Council on the Misuse of Drugs.[9] This report advocated a problem drug-taking approach to treatment, as an alternative to addiction-as disease-models. This involved an array of specialist and non-specialist services intervening to help people not only with addiction or drug issues, but also by helping them to resolve other personal, social, and family matters. The report recommended that drug services be organised through community drug teams, linking in with both specialist clinics, on the one hand, but also with mainstream primary care services, on the other.

Unlike the disease model's single focus on addiction, the community model conceived, as with alcohol, a spectrum of drug-related issues of which addiction — or 'dependency' — was one.[10] We saw it applying an eclectic mix of health perspectives with abstinence and controlled, or reduced, drug taking as appropriate treatment aims. It had a diversity of psychosocial interventions, depending on the particular circumstances.[11]

In addition, cases could be co-managed with other community professionals: health services, social work and youth services. Ideally, we saw these interventions as integrating with education, employment, social and community services, as well as health care.[12] The central purpose of this evolving model was to ensure that people who continue to use drugs problematically — whether or not they had a dependency — had access to health and social care, harm reduction measures such as needle exchange and to methadone maintenance programmes, as required. Moreover, this access was best provided by local services with the involvement of generic as well as drug specialist professionals.

The prospects of developing this model, however, were over-ambitious due mainly to the lack of community projects and services in the field we could link into. The view also among community-based professionals was that they preferred a specialist treatment system. Deference to the decision-making of specialist services such as the National Drugs Advisory and Treatment Council (NDATC) was a given. For some time, in the absence of comprehensive drug treatment, Ana Liffey and other emerging projects and services had, as stated, no alternative service system to slot into. The clinical side had little interest in working closely with outreach services. We ploughed on as if a virtual alternative was in place however, because it allowed us to argue for it as we dealt with individual caseload issues, particularly in child welfare cases.

A standard child welfare intervention arising from parental drug use, for example, was to seek evidence including from urine tests, of adherence to a drug-free regime to avert or modify statutory child care proceedings. In some circumstances, our assessment was that the drug-free bar was too high, unrealistic and likely to result in failure. If methadone programmes could achieve the stabilisation required, we argued, they should be used. This approach ran counter to the NDATC mindset, at the time the only health agency administering methadone. But once the child welfare authority — the health board — accepted an alternative plan in individual situations, it had no option but to put in place an arrangement for methadone, not through the NDATC, but through its own clinical network. Through this and other case management influences, in other services, an alternative methadone treatment regime took off.

The general situation eventually changed[13] amid a growing concern about HIV infections from sharing drug injection equipment and the obvious need for methadone programmes not tied to detoxification.[14] In the late 1980s, the health authorities employed HIV outreach workers in the AIDS Resource Centre, in Baggot Street Hospital. They were permitted to distribute condoms and later needles to targeted at-risk groups.[15] It is instructive that the health board's first significant direct investment into outreach was to employ HIV rather than drug workers. The move underlined that their main concern was not with drug use per se, but with the prospect that those injecting might transmit HIV into the wider non-drug-using, heterosexual community via unprotected sexual activity. Given that over 50% of those testing positive for HIV were intravenous drug users, it was recognised the services had to be taken 'into the streets because that is where the problem is'.[16]

Health problems arising from HIV were overwhelming and during this period there were several deaths inside and outside prison. These were from overdoses, suicides and deaths arising from AIDS and other illnesses, especially as therapeutics for AIDS were underdeveloped. One week a service user would come to Ana Liffey and engage intensely with a staff member or other service users in the kitchen or sitting room. A week or two later news could arrive about their death. In Mountjoy Prison, inmates with drug histories were tested for HIV and those with the virus were unnecessarily segregated into a separation unit. This action breached confidentiality and led to a sense of isolation and victimisation for prisoners and their families'.[17] The move reinforced stigma, encouraging a widespread negative and blaming public attitude towards those with HIV and AIDS.

Ana Liffey staff regularly — often weekly — attended funerals and spent time in clients' homes. In hospitals, they offered advice, comfort and assistance to family members outside intensive care units. It was particularly distressing when, early on in the AIDS crisis, bodybags were used just after death thus denying family members and others the opportunity for a normal grieving process. At times the project's drop-in area was akin to a funeral wake. Attendees often feared being seen openly at friends' funerals so they came to the centre which 'became a place for grieving, for mourning; a place where people have come to sympathise, to share stories about the departed and to seek new ways for both giving and receiving support'.[18] Some individuals spoke about their fears of death and continued living.

When I reflect on that period, I believe the trauma of many attending Ana Liffey had immense impact. It greatly affected the project's small staff and workers in other addiction centres along with youth and community projects. Notwithstanding the pain some people using drugs had caused others, their own lives had been severely damaged by childhood adversities and heavy teenage drug use. They suffered further because

The Harm Done

of the state's failure to respond to their plight with effective stable drug services and its persistent inability to develop a coherent policy towards treatment and social integration. They felt hugely pressurised by their families and neighbours. It is virtually impossible today to countenance or explain how these distressed predicaments had become so normalised or how utterly dysfunctional the health service was on the drug problem. State responses — especially through the separation unit — frequently exacerbated people's trauma.

By 1990, frontline staff working with heroin users, exasperated by the lack of policy progress, began to focus more directly on trying to change Government policy rather than service delivery in individual cases. Along with the addiction studies course in Trinity College, Ana Liffey organised a well-attended public meeting on new policy options for responding to drug problems in 1990. Speakers were medical and social services professionals, including from Edinburgh, who had experienced a heroin crisis similar to Dublin's in low income housing estates. But health professionals in Edinburgh had acted more quickly in reaching out to people and developing a 'localised, medically based approach to drug treatment' within a model of 'primary care' — ie community care — that included 'prescribing oral alternatives'.[19] Tellingly, neither the dominant treatment providers or health authority representatives attended the Trinity College public meeting.

It was the first meeting of its type — a gathering where alternative harm reduction and community approaches were openly advocated. The interest displayed during the discussion clearly demonstrated a broad appetite for policy change. The meeting's proceedings were published and widely circulated, helping to create a momentum towards demanding change.[20] The document set out a case for community drug treatment and community teams.[21] It gave a broad definition of 'problem drug users'[22] as an alternative to the concept of addiction. The case for community drug treatment as an 'untried response' was made at a later stage.[23] Gradually, through the 1990s the community model gained traction. It has been embraced by national drug strategies ever since the late 1990s.

Immediately after the public meeting a Drug Workers' Forum was established.[24] Although it never became a functional organisation, its members managed through inter-agency discussions and meetings with policy makers to generate considerable momentum on the need for policy changes. At the time, Ana Liffey invested in promoting a Development Group of service users who advocated directly on their own behalf for service improvements.[25] At one stage, it organised a weekend workshop in a Bray, Co Wicklow, hotel where with the assistance of frontline personnel from statutory and voluntary drug treatment agencies, they explored and developed ideas on how, as a group, they could impress on policy makers the need for change.

Along with external community and drug workers, project staff helped set up a support group, Le Chéile, for parents whose children had either died or were dying from AIDS as a result of drug use and who then felt stigmatised.[26] Most were already parenting grandchildren. They felt unsupported by mainstream authorities in the child-rearing tasks they were undertaking and their own grief.

Members of the Development Group and Le Chéile contributed to a live RTÉ radio show broadcast mid-morning from the project. They articulated the need for policy change for drug treatment and related matters.[27] Although media had previously interviewed drug users and their family members these tended to focus on the impact of drugs on their personal lives whereas this live broadcast was probably the first occasion where the focus was on policy issues and the need for change.

Subsequently, members of the Development Group had face-to-face meetings with health policy makers to explain the pitfalls of drug treatment as then structured and outlined the need for alternative models. In my ongoing dealings with department officials for the project, it was obvious they at last accepted there was a need for change. This was particularly because they realised the seriousness of HIV transmission due to intravenous drug use and following meetings with service users. They also acknowledged the need to change the health board's management arrangements. A single administrator with little evidence of internal clinical input had overall management responsibility for drugs. There was a reliance therefore on the NDATC to point a way forward. When department officials proposed changing drug services management in the health board, it was an emphatic statement they had become more serious about change.

Even so, civil servants trod a delicate route forward. They knew that not only were mainstream treatment providers and health board managers lined up against policy change, so too were Government and government-in-waiting along with the wider public. They feared that openly advocating change might be seen as caving into ideas that could be perceived politically and publicly as too liberal. Officials pursued a nuanced approach and the new 1991 *Government Strategy to Prevent Drug Misuse*[28] advocated both harm reduction and abstinence approaches. Unexpectedly, some proposals outlined in the Ana Liffey document were incorporated into this statement.

The Harm Done

While the Government's new strategy document was welcomed, it added further confusion for many operating in the field since it seemed both approaches were to be separately managed, and in general an in-depth discussion of drug policy options was eschewed. Abstinence had well established institutional supports, resources and personnel that could now be strengthened. In contrast, harm reduction work initially consisted of a small team of public health staff and HIV outreach workers unsure if they had political and administrative cover for their work on the ground. In the wake of the new strategy document, an AIDS / Drugs Coordinator — a public health professional, Joe Barry — was assigned to the Eastern Health Board to put together new initiatives. For some time, though, the funding to support Barry's proposals fell short of what was required.

Behind the scenes and out of the public gaze, a deeper transformation was in train. It was guided in the main by continuing public health concerns around HIV / AIDS and an acceptance by health officials, following a submission to Government by the Irish College of General Practitioners, that GPs should have a mainstream role in treatment of opiate addiction to stem the spread of HIV infection.[29] A small group of senior officials and public health professionals planned an adjustment to the legislation achieved by way of statutory instrument (thus without Dáil debate). Later known as the Methadone Protocol it established a basis for the involvement — and payment — of GPs in prescribing the drug.

The protocol consolidated a centralised system for methadone prescribing and offered considerable flexibility for family doctors and community pharmacists willing to work directly with opiate-dependent clients. Simultaneously it offered safeguards against multiple prescribing for individual drug users and so reduced the risk of methadone leakage into a black market. Previously, the 1986 *First Report of the National Coordinating Committee on Drug Abuse* expressed concern about the 'irresponsible prescribing' of methadone, but offered no prospect for assigning GPs a role in addiction treatment.[30] Clearly with the methadone protocol a lot had changed.

While welcomed by frontline service providers, the changes were an example of behind-the-scenes policy making: no open debate, no public consultation. Instead it was a coming together of key decision-makers and medical practitioners determined to get a job done and to introduce methadone treatment regardless of institutional resistance.[31] It was a good example of the barriers facing policy makers with a public health agenda. Yet the decision was hardly good for an open democracy. It reflected the inability of public health leaders to confront and debate these issues openly as they did, for example, during the Covid-19 pandemic.

As they set about establishing treatment facilities in local communities, health officials provoked residents' opposition. This was due at times to a failure to consult with and open up negotiation with local groups that included former advocates of methadone provision who had expected involvement in setting them up. While health officials had a new policy, they were sometimes unsure how to communicate it or garner community support for its implementation or how to build service-user enthusiasm. The idea of engaging grassroots bodies in developing and implementing the change was new. There was community opposition to proposals to roll-out methadone facilities and needle exchange schemes in the north inner city[32], Blanchardstown and Cork Street.[33] Indeed, a few years later there was a fire at a health centre in Tallaght amid local protests against methadone provision.[34] It was clear that a model of community consultation was needed to achieve the roll-out.

The changed attitude towards harm reduction services gradually made it easier for the Ana Liffey Drug Project and similar services to secure some basic state funds to continue their own brand of low threshold outreach and treatment. There was still no substantial official acknowledgement, however, that because the problems were concentrated mainly in specific geographic neighbourhoods, a consultation and engagement alongside substantial community investment, was essential for implementation. This came later.

In 1990, Community Response in the south inner city emerged as a campaign group around drugs. Social worker Michael Lacey, along with other health board professionals in Community Care Area 3, played an important role in leading this initiative which brought together personnel from across the spectrum in community, voluntary and statutory bodies. They aimed to get an across-the-board agreement on how to tackle drug problems. I got involved with the group through Ana Liffey as we were active in building alliances with community organisations and community-based professional groups, such as social workers and a newly emerging group of AIDS / HIV outreach workers.

Significantly, Community Response was not dominated by any single vested interest and had success in bringing the drug issue into wider political and policy domains. In November 1990, it organised a well-attended conference in the College of Technology, Kevin Street (now Technological University Dublin) that attracted a diverse mix of senior gardaí, health care personnel, lawyers, youth and community workers, and local people — including people previously involved in anti-drug actions.[35] In April 1991, it presented its ideas to Dublin City Council's monthly meeting.[36] It was the second time in ten years I had been asked to speak at a council meeting. This time I noticed there was a change in councillor members. Some comments remained the same as before. The councillors agreed to refer the matter to a youth sub-committee amidst an admission that the council could do little about the drug problem in the absence of a reform in drug policy.

In outlining its background and context, Community Response in a report on its conference published in 1991, stated that after a decade of variable responses people had to come together to develop a unified, partnership approach.[37] It subsequently mobilised local support for neighbourhood-based methadone facilities and prevention programmes. In later years, it reorganised itself as an important drug and alcohol service in the south inner city, where it continues to have an influential role to this day.[38]

Four years later in the north inner city, social worker Fergus McCabe was instrumental in establishing Citywide. Like Community Response, this was a partnership group that united community workers, trade unionists, and personnel from voluntary and statutory agencies all focused on bringing about new treatment policies and other changes.[39] It later became a resource agency for community organisations throughout the city involved with drug issues.[40]

Similar new community initiatives took place in Killinarden, Tallaght, where CARP (Community Addiction Response Programme) formed in 1995 and set up its own methadone prescribing facility with help from a private GP.[41] This arrangement created leverage for securing state support for clinical services. It continues to exist with mainstream funding, alongside other local prescribing facilities that emerged around the same time in other parts of Tallaght.[42]

Following the *Government Strategy to Prevent Substance Misuse* (1991), a pilot community drug team formed in Rialto.[43] Along with health board social worker Eibhlín O'Loingsigh, I was among those asked to oversee its work on a management group under the auspices of the Rialto Development Association. As well as creating frontline services for drug users and family members — counselling, personal development, assertiveness training, harm reduction and access to methadone maintenance — the Rialto Community Drug Team (RCDT), hosted regular community forums to engage community members and local bodies. In this way it countered 'negative rumours and misconceptions' thereby ensuring it had a positive strategy for engaging with potential 'objectors' to its work.[44] Early on, it emphasised demystifying methadone and prescribing issues, thus building credibility and legitimacy for its work.

This was important given the potential for positive and negative community responses (see Introduction) to proposals for new local services. As mentioned above, there had been local protests against siting community methadone facilities in other locations. To support engagement, RCDT recruited a community drug worker whose role was to maintain contact with key local bodies and community members and develop initiatives such as family support groups, bereavement programmes for children, and educational programmes.

At the outset, RCDT along with the local youth project hosted a remembrance service, Friends Remembering Friends, for those who had died as a result of drug use, particularly AIDS-related illnesses, and produced two plays on this theme. These events followed by several similar activities since, helped consolidate the group as an integrated community project. By 1996, it had created the 'conditions for supporting problem drug users in their own neighbourhoods' despite Government lack of progress in introducing a comprehensive harm reduction framework, as promised five years earlier.[45]

Elsewhere, local treatment service groups were self-established with similar results. These included Clondalkin Addiction Support Project (CASP) (1995) and Addiction Response Crumlin (ARC) (1996). Together these services and initiatives added to a growing demand that Government policy on harm reduction needed proper local structures and resources for implementation.

In 1996, following the IRA killing of Detective Garda Jerry McCabe (1943–96) in Limerick, and the murder by members of John Gilligan's drugs gang of crime journalist Veronica Guerin (1959–96), in Dublin, the Irish government came under unprecedented public, media and political pressure to develop new anti-crime and anti-drug strategies. On the drug supply side, the government strengthened policing and security measures, and also introduced the Criminal Assets Bureau Act (1986) — which established a successful scheme for seizing the property of suspected criminals — including drug dealers — who were required to prove that their private assets were not from the proceeds of crime.

A new ministerial committee was formed to look at drug demand side issues. Four months later, in October, it published the *First Report of the Ministerial Task Force on Measures to Reduce the Demand for Drugs*.[46] Often referred to as the Rabbitte Report because its chair was Junior Minister Pat Rabbitte, a man familiar with local drug issues through his Tallaght constituency, the report set out a strategy for dealing with drug problems from the demand perspective.[47] It recommended putting into place local drug task force partnership bodies in the most affected areas.

It introduced a budget and management system to ensure drug-related treatment and prevention initiatives were devised and implemented through local structures. In the spirit of the Government's Strategic Management Initiative that proposed inter alia that 'interacting Departmental strategies should be coordinated'[48] a cross-departmental structure emerged for overseeing and giving direction to drug initiatives. Following public consultation Government published a National Drug Strategy incorporating supply and demand issues in 2001.[49] This has been updated twice since in 2009 (National Drugs Strategy, 2009–16)[50] and 2017 (National Drugs Strategy, 2017–25).[51]

These changes constituted a major shift in policy, especially as they were accompanied by substantial funds. Methadone prescribing and clinical facilities for needle sharing gathered momentum. A young people's facilities fund was created and utilised to introduce a wide range of targeted preventative programmes and facilities into disadvantaged communities. The overall effort aimed to help deal, in a focused manner, with the close association between heroin use and socio-economic disadvantage, an approach so patently avoided and institutionally undermined in earlier decades.

When the heroin problem emerged and escalated in the late 1970s, there should have been a national centrally-led political debate on drug policies, prevention and other interventions, and their social and economic context. The initial period was characterised by denial and a failure to act, amid suppression of dialogue and marginalisation of community groups and individuals trying to raise awareness of what was unfolding in senior levels of healthcare, Government and broader domains.

In retrospect, given the early evidence of needle-sharing and hepatitis infections it is difficult to find a coherent explanation for health leaders' inability to get on top of the emerging problem. In later years it has been suggested the authorities were taken by surprise and had no external models for guidance. This position is only partly credible. It does not explain the length of time it took to reframe policies. More plausibly, inherent conservatism prevented them from acknowledging a mounting drug crisis with a social dimension.

A search for solutions required a significant change in the then dominant mindset that held individual pathology as a cause for drug issues. Instead during the early 1980s, authorities courted close relationships with organisations that supported an individualised analysis of heroin problems devoid of social context. Anyone who tried to frame the problem differently was seen as well-meaning but naïve. Meanwhile there was a failure, initially, to grasp the opportunities presented by engagement with service initiatives such as the Ana Liffey Drug Project that operated low threshold, outreach drop-in facilities on a shoestring. Since the mid 1990s such interventions are now commonplace in local communities.

With the Rabbitte Report, Government finally accepted and started delivering on the unpublished recommendations for community priority area schemes made by the 1983 Special Governmental Task Force on Drugs. Thirteen long years awaiting.

A workshop on detached work with youth-at-risk, in DLR Drug and Alcohol Task Force, 2017.
Photo: Barry Cullen

Mairéad Grennan, Practice Liaison Worker and John Doyle, Acting Coordinator, DLR Drug and Alcohol Task Force, 2023.
Photo: Barry Cullen

CHAPTER 9

Not All Plain Sailing for Task Forces

Twenty-seven years after the Rabbitte Report (see Chapter 8), it can be justifiably stated that things are significantly different. New local services ensure that, in the main, drug users have previously unavailable options for mitigation and treatment. National strategies largely succeeded in dealing with drug problems, specifically heroin. A high point in marking early progress was a 2005 conference, Vital Connections — Leading the Response, organised by the network of chairs and coordinators from local drug task forces. Workshops and papers from multiple perspectives across different statutory, voluntary and community agencies were included. Together, these illustrated the shift from the exclusive abstinence model of a decade earlier to the community model. It demonstrated an ability to identify key cross-sectoral areas of achievement as well as new challenges ahead.[1]

When the conference was held there was optimism about consolidating the community approach and preparing for the next phase in national planning. In particular, new evidence was emerging — reflecting evaluation developments in the UK[2] and elsewhere[3] — that improving access to methadone maintenance could reduce rates of HIV infection and drug-related behaviours of those in treatment.[4]

The impact of the new community model is especially evident in that the numbers of young people — under 25 years — who presented for methadone treatment fell from 60%[5] of the total in the mid-1990s to 13.6% of first presentations in 2021, (with less than 1% of those currently presenting under 18 years).[6] A HSE project, YODA[7], set up in the mid 2000s in response to the then perceived need for a clinically-led methadone service for under eighteens[8] experienced a fall-off in demand in a few years of being established. The project stopped operating its heroin-based service completely in 2018, contending that a 95% national decline in adolescent heroin addiction was achieved by altering Ireland's overall treatment response.[9]

While these treatment changes undoubtedly had impact, other factors potentially had more importance. For example, targeted prevention interventions undertaken jointly by task forces, youth / community drug and out-of-school services, helped to divert younger at-risk cohorts from choosing and being involved with heroin. Several young people — across society — continued to use cannabis, alcohol and other drugs although it became clear that at-risk groups were mainly avoiding opiates. Another factor in the shift from heroin was an economic uplift that offered an improved outlook for some of the most affected communities and their young members.

The Dún Laoghaire Rathdown (DLR) Drug and Alcohol Task Force with which I worked as coordinator in 2013–21 is one example of the array of activities supported through the community model.[10] As well as undertaking ongoing research, community consultation and analysis of the area's changing needs and strategic planning, the task force offered financial support in three specific service areas: community treatment, family support, and youth prevention.

The task force established the Community Addiction Team in 1997 and today all its staff are trained and accredited in motivational assessment and community reinforcement therapies.[11] They have an area-based referral and intake system and offer a once-off, twelve-session, individually customised programme to help participants assert control over alcohol or drug use. Follow-up group support, counselling and other after-care supports are also available. Separately the HSE provides clinical facilities for methadone prescribing through a local medical centre and designated GPs. It also funds a daily attendance programme for those opting for intensive drug-free rehabilitation.[12]

On the family support side, the task force has interventions in place to support families of adult members whose substance misuse is impinging on family welfare.[13] A separate family programme is in place to support children negatively impacted by parental drug or alcohol use.[14] In targeted youth prevention, various local bodies supply counselling, education and group supports for young people at high risk of substance misuse.[15]

Inter-agency structures help contribute to early identification of emerging needs. These are then deliberated on amid plans and funding arrangements for new developments. For example, initiatives around Hidden Harms, Youth-At-Risk Network and Collaborative Training arose from such deliberations.[16] Similar sets of programmes were developed in other task force areas. Given the obvious differences in local and geographic context, the structure and focus of such programmes vary.[17]

It has not been all plain sailing for task forces or local community projects, however. Following the launch of the National Drugs Strategy 2009–16[18], public expenditure cutbacks due to the banking collapse and recession took their toll on all community and social services, locally and nationally. Several of the strategy's envisaged initiatives were not implemented and virtually all existing measures experienced cuts. In 2008–14 the task forces coped with year-on-year budgetary reductions (30% over the period). Ten years later (2023) their funding remained fixed at 2013 levels even though overall health spending had risen by 42% during 2014–21.[19] A small cost-of-living percentage increase was agreed in 2023, but it will have little impact given the years of financial cutback, especially as community project staff lost pay parity with health board workers following the recession.

The retrenchment has had a significant impact on plans to develop new rehabilitation services especially. The need for them was a concern during the consultations leading to the National Drug Strategy 2009–16 that was drafted against a background of intense consideration of the issue.[20] A distinction was made between treatment and rehabilitation and the new strategy adopted the latter as a fifth component (pillar), in addition to supply, prevention, treatment and research. This distinction put the spotlight on developing interventions focused specifically on assisting individuals to recover from addiction when desired, as opposed to those such as methadone often perceived as tending to help people maintain a safe level of opiate use.

Concerns about rehabilitation and recovery are continually expressed and generate public and parliamentary questions on methadone's sustainability.[21] Legislators are fearful of funding such programmes if it leads to accusations that public funds are being used to support addiction. Thus it is often claimed that people are on methadone for too long, spurring a demand to get users off drugs, off methadone, out of medical treatment and working towards drug-free recovery. Many observers remain wedded to the belief that recovery means abstinent, 'moved on' from methadone and assisted to achieve a new status through residential detoxification facilities.[22] Perhaps inadvertently, a harking back to the old abstinent ideas is being aired.[23]

Some criticisms of methadone provision are well-founded, especially as the previous specialist clinical system for the disease model has to an extent been replicated within community-based settings.[24] Stigma is often reinforced by well-intentioned efforts to deliver more specialist services thus reinforcing difference. In creating a system where those dependent on heroin could access methadone quickly, the new arrangements have existed in parallel to mainstream health and social services with little planned integration between both. An example would be lack of consideration for integrating drug services into newly-established primary care centres. Integration is not simply about co-locating methadone and psycho-social services, but ensuring people who need methadone access it the same way as people access other medications.

Most people on methadone receive their prescriptions not from the network of thousands of community-based GPs and pharmacies as would be expected for other chronic conditions, but from specialist community clinics not necessarily pursuing an integration policy. On its own, methadone does not achieve social integration. It works best in achieving stability or normality when accompanied — as previously mentioned — by psychosocial therapies and normal community supports.

In 2018, conscious that the community model had not succeeded in the expected widespread reintegration of drug users into society and that the issue of ageing drug users had been raised at a European level[25], the DLR task force commissioned Trinity College Dublin to undertake research on the needs of older drug users on long-term methadone.[26] The outcome showed that they continued to lack social integration[27], and faced serious stigmatisation, isolation, and ongoing poor outcomes because of their situation.[28] The research illustrated respondents' concerns about supervised urine testing, abandoned in recent years only after considerable external pressure especially by the service users' group SURIA (Service Users Rights in Action).[29]

An important consideration in discussion on the viability of methadone provision on the one hand and demands for more rehabilitation programmes on the other is this: there is no magic bullet for getting people off drugs. The problem — drug dependence or drug addiction — cannot be cured in a classical clinical sense. No preset formula or set of procedures exists. As mentioned on a few occasions in this book, abstinence is rarely attainable, particularly with illegally acquired opiates. Many drug users have few human resources — well-functioning family relationships, educational attainments, housing security and a clean bill of health with the criminal justice system — considered vital to overcoming these problems, resources that offer the best protection for people at risk of substance misuse in the first instance.

Perhaps, the most significant development to come out of rehabilitation debates was the incorporation, in 2011, of an integrated care planning and case management framework — *National Rehabilitation Framework Document* — in operating drug services.[30] This framework is focused on creating individual rehabilitation pathways to ensure 'individuals affected by drug misuse are offered a range of integrated options tailored to meet their needs'[31] and in accordance with a four-tiered system — spanning primary, secondary, specialist and intensive care systems — for managing such problems.

Theoretically, the tiered framework envisages users entering (or re-entering) treatment / rehabilitation at levels that match the seriousness of their problems at any one time. Interventions are assumed to be multi-faceted and operating across a range of psychosocial modalities depending on the individual's level of problems, engagement with change and the overall complexity of their relationships and living situations.

Shortcomings became evident within the framework's proposed roll-out, however, in 2011. As already mentioned, this was shortly after promised funding was not delivered due to financial cutbacks after the banking collapse and recession of 2009-14. Without money the framework foundered.

The framework furthermore, was premised on effective collaboration between clinical and non-clinical treatment professionals, few of whom had significant previous experience of or training in collaboration. This shortcoming was significant and continues to inhibit progress in framework implementation. Even had funding been available there would be scepticism about the capacities of clinical and non-clinical personnel to engage meaningfully in collaborative practices.

In addition, whatever model is used to frame recovery — be it the abstinence model, the community approach or harm reduction — the legal position remains the overriding obstacle in drug takers' journeys towards normality. Illicit-drugs users have, by definition, disobeyed the rules. Irrespective of the health and social impact on them personally of their behaviours, the policy mainstay is to label it as deviant and they as transgressors.

In general, society holds sympathetic views on drug users and their rights of access to treatment. Nonetheless, they have been perceived as irresponsible and a threat.[32] Most people given a choice would not wish to live close to or associate with someone addicted to drugs.[33] Negativity towards them contributes to a scapegoating, for instance arising from anti-social activities in city centre locations, where the tendency is to

The Harm Done

blame drug users while paying little attention to the troubles caused by alcohol abuse.

Delays in developing harm reduction facilities, especially drug-injection rooms reflect this negativity. International reviews are generally positive about the role of such sites in reducing overdose morbidity and mortality, improving injecting behaviours and in access to treatment facilities. They report little or no impact on crime or public nuisance[34] and their benefits outweigh the risks.[35] The lack of progress in developing such facilities in Dublin, points to a continued public negativity towards drug users related, one assumes, to the legal issue. In this regard, drug-takers' health and social care are widely considered subordinate to legal control. So while the current National Drugs Strategy, 2017–25[36] is framed as a health-led response, for as long as drug users continue to be criminalised general aims of social integration remain distant and for most unattainable. The effective operation of a health-led strategy requires an untangling of the prohibition mindset (see Chapter 10).

In addition to the lack of progress since 2009 in developing rehabilitation services, other developments have had an impact on the community model's viability. National structures previously in place to support the activities of task forces were, in the absence of new national funding, paused and effectively decommissioned. With little central direction and only one small increase in their core funding since before 2008, local bodies have lacked the resources and essential capacity-building supports to make themselves more effective and responsive. This has hampered their ability to address existing and emerging problems and to reach out to involve community members in their activities. As a result, they are at significant risk of stagnation. They and the various services and networks they support will require major overhaul and reorganisation as well as investment if they are to reclaim their previous position of leading drug policy debates and changes.

The cutbacks had a particularly negative impact on the current National Drugs Strategy, 2017–25. This was formulated by a recession mindset even though the recession had by then passed. Once the plan was published, it was clear that centralised, specialist interests would have a greater say in driving new ventures and whatever new funding became available.[37] With responsibility for drug policy back in the Department of Health[38], the planning model has shifted towards service uniformity across large health area populations of about 250,000 or more, under the direction of nine Community Health Organisations (CHOs), in line with Sláinte Care. Thus the operational strategy around drugs within each area relied on respective managerial commitments, alongside regional drug strategies.

In CHO4 (Cork / Kerry), for example, there is reportedly a strong regional structure for a planned, integrated drug strategy, thereby ensuring that drug services operate alongside and in conjunction with primary care and mental health services.[39] In contrast in CHO6 (Dublin South-East / DLR / West Wicklow), there is no HSE regional structure for drugs or managerial involvement at all in drug services, and thus no possibility of integration with other CHO6 services. Indeed, management responsibility for CHO6 falls to CHO7 (Kildare West Wicklow / Dublin West / Dublin South City / Dublin South West), already dealing with the greatest burden nationally of drug problems and funded services, with responsibility for seven task force areas: Ballyfermot, Clondalkin, Canal Communities, Crumlin / Kimmage, south inner city, Tallaght and Dublin south west / Kildare.

The new Sláinte Care arrangements look great on a slide show, where regional structures have standard populations and relatively evenly-distributed needs. In practice, the model fails to account for highly variable needs within smaller, mainly urban areas, where needs are concentrated within particular localities and among particular groups. The new model appears as a return to doing business as previously during the 1980s, when the central structure was ascendant, and when the attitude of the health authorities, as the heroin problem emerged in inner city communities, was that they could not act until they had a single, universal plan for the whole country or region. Sláinte Care potentially works well with mainstream and everyday health issues, but not for problems that are unevenly distributed. With this new regional model on the rise, the omens were there: the community model, that had at least brought some degree of partnerships at local levels, was in retreat.[40]

Paradoxically, most task forces would acknowledge the model needs renewal. Certainly, this aspect was one that I found challenging when I was coordinator of the DLR task force in 2013–21. At times it was difficult to reconcile my understanding of a task force as a short-lived entity with its twenty-seven year lifespan. My first introduction to the task force idea was the Task Force on Child Care Services, 1974–80.[41] That task force began deliberating in 1974 and issued an interim report in 1975. Its final report was comprehensive and once submitted in 1980, the task force ceased to exist.

The premise for establishing local drug task forces in Dublin in 1996 was the need to focus, through a collaborative process, the resources and energies of relevant agencies and Government departments on specific geographic areas where drug problems, particularly heroin, were concentrated. The geographic features have substantially changed in the twenty-seven years since they were first established. Several inner city flat complexes have been either demolished or substantially regenerated, as meanwhile vast tracts of privately rented estates with unquantified needs have emerged on Dublin's periphery, and are not directly covered by local task forces.

There can be little doubting that a reconfiguring of basic and relative needs is needed alongside an identification of new concentrations of drugs and related issues. The problems that gave rise to the 1996 task force may need to be reviewed in light of new developments, changing drug problems, evidence of concentrations and with attention to the need for local structures — where required — in the long-term. The title 'task force' indeed may have outlived its usefulness and need replacement, but local structures — where there is evidence of a concentration of drug-related problems — however described, are still needed.

In addition, the internal tasks of these bodies also need to be addressed. When I started working as coordinator in DLR Drug and Alcohol Task Force in 2013, fourteen separate projects were being funded through task force supports, with very little evidence of coordination or integration. In reviewing the work, we settled on three separate funding strands: a treatment agency, family support and youth prevention. Directing funds to services to deliver on these strands inevitably required a winding-down of funds from some existing bodies. Organisationally, there were significant challenges in bringing about the changes that were required, not least being the need to ensure such proposals had the complete support of task force members, including those who represented communities and political representatives. As mentioned earlier politicians don't like closing things, and often prefer to see available resources distributed across a number of organisations rather than strategically positioned in one or two places. In some instances, they relish the opportunity to use closures as a rallying call. Thankfully, in this instance, the public representatives alongside others on the task force rose to the challenge of making strategic decisions.

As is evident from discussions elsewhere in this book a range of models exists to overcome drug problems. In my view, while personal motivation, will-power and self-regulation are key to an individual taking control of their drug use, the external supports and scaffolding that help hold people together — physically and psychologically — are equally important. Many succeed in their endeavours, some by becoming abstinent, some by being maintained on alternative drugs and others by finding various mechanisms such as fellowships, mutual support groups, occasional counselling and so forth to help them put shape and direction on their lives.

The most viable scaffolding is that provided through families and communities, and thus the availability and coordination of state-supported family and community services play an essential role in facilitating people's journeys. A basic requirement is that these supports are built around the encouragement of self-management and social integration and with ongoing attention to developing relevant community-based interventions as required. If built around coercion and control, or if they are underpinned by the notion that a standalone specialist clinician, counsellor, or therapist can determine a person's destiny, or that adherence to a fixed ideologically constructed model, or legal model indeed, is required, such services inevitably fail.

Typically, different combinations of approaches are used or alternatively the same approach can be used 'at different points in the therapeutic pathway.'[42] The essential ingredient in ensuring that different interventions have impact does not lie in the techniques and methodologies of different services. Instead they lie in their capacities and willingness to view the issues systemically, to work in partnership with other bodies and ensure the drug users they work with have access to a wraparound approach, integrating specialist drug treatments with non-specialist, generic services. Whether the model is directed nationally, regionally or locally, the existence of a reliable community structure, such as a task force, is essential to achieving its operation.

Attendance at Addiction Research Centre conference in Trinity College in 2000
Photo: Derek Speirs ©

Julian Cohen and Mary Cullen speakers at Addiction Research Conference, Trinity College 2006
Photo: Derek Speirs ©

CHAPTER 10

Changing the 'Unchangeable' Drug Laws

In previous pages I have set out Ireland's diverging opinions and perspectives on how best to deal with drugs in society. At times, policies have become deeply divisive with some practice options generating considerable opposition. The absence of an ongoing centrally-led rational debate certainly has not helped matters. Worth nothing in this regard, perhaps, is the introduction without public debate of the Methadone Protocol (see Chapter 8): a national conversation beforehand might well have scuppered it. Public debate around safe-injecting facilities began in 2015 and legislation for safe injection sites was passed in 2017. Six years later there are none.

During the first phase of national drug strategies in 2001–09, general enthusiasm gave rise to several open discussions on drug issues, including the conference Vital Connections, organised by local drug task forces in 2005.[1] In addition, the children's and addiction research centres, in Trinity College where I was based, 1995–2011, hosted a series of public debates and annual conferences (1997–2006) around drugs, alcohol, and related matters. These had large attendances, with a wide range of international researchers and policy experts, as well as domestic speakers.[2]

An early event in 1997[3], one year after the Rabbitte report, heard speakers argue that many drug-related societal problems arose mainly from the failure to distinguish between problem drug use concerned with persons who as a result need treatment, and others 'who use cannabis and / or other illicit drugs on an experimental or ongoing recreational basis' where no treatment is required.[4] The tone of this seminar was optimistic about opening a debate on young people's drug use. It reflected

The Harm Done

a constructive outlook within Government during the period after the formation of local drug task forces and preparations for developing national drug strategies. A willingness was evident among officials who were involved in emerging national structures to debate these matters, not to be constrained by the legal issue, thus drugs could be discussed as normal even though they were prohibited.

Speaker Howard Parker, co-author of *Illegal Leisure*[5] — a report on a longitudinal study of adolescent drug use in northwest England — emphasised that society was moving towards a normalisation of recreational drug use as a 'long term feature of youth culture' that would not simply 'go away in the foreseeable future'. The developing drug scene, he claimed, would most likely include 'high levels of drugs knowledge among young people, extensive drug-trying' and 'accommodation of recreational drug use within youth culture'.[6] *Illegal Leisure* included a cohort of young people from the post-heroin generation and what was remarkable was that researchers discovered little difference in young people's drug-taking behaviours across class and gender. Significant numbers across all groups were using cannabis and amphetamines.

Other speakers from key service and policy agencies emphasised the challenge of shifting the narrative around drugs away from the heroin-only perspective and also from moving away 'from only seeing drug-taking as a criminal activity, a social problem or an illness'. During the conference, there was a strong expectation that energies could be steered in the direction of a policy overhaul, amidst hopes that government would establish a statutory advisory group on drugs to debate and analyse these issues in the same manner perhaps as the Uk's Advisory Council Misuse of Drugs (ACMD). The optimism was short-lived however. Although a National Advisory Committee on Drugs was established, it did not have statutory independence and its research programme was underpinned mainly by a consideration of epidemiological and implementation issues around drugs, with little exploration of alternative models.

In a later Trinity College conference in 2002 on drugs and crime, speaker Tim Murphy, author of *Re-thinking the War on Drugs*[7] highlighted that while most stakeholders had by then embraced harm reduction, this did not unfortunately include much support for examining recreational drug use or relaxing the laws for controlling drug supply. The demand for harm reduction, he argued, arose from a very fraught heroin problem that had devastated communities. Many people were still trying en masse to get over it. Yet drug-related crime, he maintained, arose mainly from drug prohibition. Driving the market underground created community disorganisation which affected 'the norms and behaviours of individuals who live in the community'. They are also 'associated with increases in crime that are not directly related to drug selling'.[8] In Murphy's analysis, the heroin problem as then experienced (see Chapter 3) could be traced not only to changes in global supply, market opportunities and social exclusion, but, perhaps more importantly, to prohibition, to the laws that apply — national and international — laws that had a direct impact on destabilising and marginalising communities.

Murphy's arguments and his invitation to focus on the need to debate prohibition policy generated little interest. The wide-ranging audience was more preoccupied with ensuring drug prevention, methadone maintenance, rehabilitation and other measures for mitigating serious heroin problems, were introduced into places where they were most badly needed. The impetus for a renewed debate on the legal issue arose only in recent years.

When I was coordinator of the DLR Drug and Alcohol Task Force 2013-21, frontline youth and community personnel continually expressed concern about these issues. Strongly referenced was the ongoing problem of young people caught up in cannabis use and as everyday couriers in the criminal drug trade. There was a need, it was argued, to reassess the role legal prohibition played in marginalising the young people they worked with. Frustrated staff saw no research was being undertaken on young people's experiences outside that of clinical studies. Thus, they often commented that little was known about drug use among those who did not present for treatment. Their accounts did not inform clinical data.

When young people willingly came forward in DLR acknowledging their need for help in dealing with a dependency, involving the treatment services was reported as relatively straightforward. Procedures were in place to support clients at different levels and to offer them psychosocial treatment when needed. So they could see a key worker for a number of defined therapeutic sessions in a community setting. Alternatively they could be referred to a specialist service operated by the HSE. In rare circumstances, if their need for residential treatment was indicated, a procedure was in place to make this referral and for the HSE to pay for it.

But mostly matters were not so straightforward, especially when a wide gap was evident between adult and young people's perceptions. Thus only a few of the latter availed of these procedures. What many practitioners and others considered to be causing serious problems, usually because of school suspension, was increasingly viewed by some young people as recreational drug use.[9] Community service providers struggled with the challenge of assigning personnel and other resources to provide and facilitate what appeared to be involuntary treatment that had little meaningful outcome. Why would we put funding into trying to treat young people who don't want and may not need treatment they asked, when we could use the resources in a more considered, respectful way with a wider group of at-risk young people?

More worryingly, they expressed concerns that many young people were functioning as street-level suppliers and couriers, being drawn deep into criminality. This, more than individual drug use, was foremost in their concerns. Research conducted in the north inner city reported that young people, instead of opting for new training and employment opportunities, were choosing the 'lucrative option of a role within the drugs trade' along with its drug-related debt and turf battles.[10] Alongside a normalisation of drug use as predicted by Howard Parker and his associates, there was a normalisation of linked criminality. Thus for individuals, families and communities continually living with contemporary drug problems, their current need was not for more treatment, but for more effective methods to deal with the everyday fear and violence caused by drug criminality and its pervasive impact on young people's lives.[11]

In 2021, these concerns were echoed by a group of over 100 youth frontline workers in youth services who, in a public statement, called for an end to drugs prohibition altogether. It 'drives our young people who use drugs underground, it isolates them and places them in danger... the policy of prohibition / criminalisation has failed and is not the way forward'.[12] One group member Eddie D'Arcy, a Dublin youth worker for over forty years, was interviewed in the *Irish Times* in 2021: 'Even enormous success in terms of (drug) seizures hasn't radically affected the gangs and it hasn't affected the level of drugs in communities... it's 'not a war we're ever going to win'.[13]

In the past, prohibition debates on the merits or otherwise of legislative reform were frequently diverted into a hopeless legally framed attitude that drugs were intrinsically bad, and evil. It is instructive, for example, that in 2006 a Joint Oireachtas Committee, having commissioned a report on the case for including alcohol in the National Drug Strategy, rejected the concluding proposal. Instead it adopted an alternative approach in which the term 'substance misuse' replaced 'drugs and alcohol'.[14]

At the last hurdle they were 'loath to have alcohol classified alongside heroin and cocaine etc, and all that entails'.[15] They objected to the idea of equating legal alcohol with illegal drugs. This episode reflected a taken-for-granted tendency to view drug use as outside 'normal' people's experience. Stigma was seen as inhering in others' individual drug behaviours. The role of societal forces was missing from the analysis. There was little tolerance of the concept of normalisation in this mindset.

So the widespread use of alcohol is accepted as normal — is something we all do — but having and using cannabis is criminalised. This despite many believing the former causes greater individual and social harms[16] and despite almost 30% of people using cannabis at some stage in their lifetime.[17] Meanwhile, the global burden of disease attributable to alcohol[18] remains greater than that for illegal drugs.[19] It is significantly higher in western societies, including Ireland.[20]

Separately in a 2006 Dáil debate the then Justice Minister Michael McDowell, in a speech describing drugs as a 'scourge' referenced the 'unchangeable European law to criminalise the possession of these drugs' as underpinning Ireland's established position.[21] McDowell concluded that any proposal to legalise drugs was 'a non-starter'.[22]

While this uncritical narrative is perceived as authoritative, internationally there are growing signs of a relaxation of the prohibitionist perspective.[23] McDowell himself revealed a more liberal view in 2023 when he stated in the Seanad: 'Adults should not be penalised for the use of cannabis in any circumstance. If they want to do that, just as if they want to drink or smoke tobacco, that is their option. From a liberal perspective I have to say that if people want to do themselves harm, and cannabis of varying strengths can be extremely harmful, that is generally their business as far as I am concerned'.[24] Meanwhile, considered calls for legalisation have been aired by the *Economist* magazine[25] the London *Times* and Royal Society of Public Health.[26] In June 2023, the Irish Labour Party rowed in publicly behind proposals for legal reform[27] and the Citizens' Assembly on Drugs Use was an opportunity for those for and against relaxation of drugs laws to submit their views.

From a pharmacological perspective, no mood-altering drug — including alcohol — is safe. Depending on their dose, mode and frequency of intake, all drugs have the capacity for toxicity and to cause illness and death, particularly through overdose poisoning. Most drugs, including alcohol, when taken in regulated amounts and under controlled conditions carry little additional risk except — in some instances — that of dependency or prolonged excessive use.

Once legalised more people will undoubtedly use drugs that are now illegal. Like alcohol, some would become dependent or overindulge causing other problems as in drug-driving, domestic violence or drug-related disease. But most — as with alcohol — would control their use

The Harm Done

with little if any wider effects. Some drinkers indeed would potentially, switch to cannabis or develop a balanced use of both: less alcohol, more cannabis.

Alcohol is a very dangerous, toxic substance that is not legally available in pure form, but in beverage. In recognising its dangers it is legally sold only in licensed, adult-only outlets having been manufactured in highly controlled fermentation and distilling. Such controls are important from a public health perspective. Inevitably the alcohol market — producers, suppliers, retailers and consumers — will continuously find ways to push back against controls and make it difficult through advertising, political lobbying and other means to prevent legislators from imposing restrictions on the sale and promotion of their products.

All currently illegal drugs, notwithstanding their toxicity and variable strengths and formulations, can potentially be prepared through similar processes as alcohol and ingested in flavoured beverages or via smoking, solid food and inhalants. The choice is endless. Like cigarettes, some drug use could take place in personal private spaces or social, small groups at house parties or club gatherings for a picnic or barbecues or a walk in the park.

In moving from a prohibitionist mindset, which will eventually happen, there is a need to envisage an alternative framework for regulating the manufacture, sale, possession and use of drugs. Under this framework, people who use drugs in a problematic manner need to be perceived — as are problem drinkers —as individuals needing help and treatment. Where ongoing drug use has little or no bearing on either their own or other people's welfare or safety, it should not unnecessarily come to the attention of either law enforcement or specialist health authorities.

Legislators will resist passing laws that lead, however unintentionally, to more people using previously banned substances. They will not want to be associated with the inevitable media outcry arising from potentially increased rates of addiction. Yet just as the opportunity to debate drug decriminalisation and legalisation gathers momentum, it seems further liberalisation and deregulation of alcohol is scheduled with little debate or discussion.[28] So far legislators have rarely expressed concern about the impact of such change on future rises in alcohol consumption and a likely rise in alcohol-related deaths and illnesses. If anything, current deficits in regulating the alcohol industry, as in the 0.0 branding debacle[29], and its well-organised ability to influence policy-making[30], are poor portents of a restrained cannabis, cocaine or opiate industry. Most likely they too would adopt alcohol industry strategies and use their substantial resources for political lobbying and public persuasion.

Logically, all drug use — including alcohol use — falls into a category that requires governments to take extraordinary actions to reduce and limit negative consequences. It was succinctly stated in the title of a seminal WHO publication that alcohol is not an ordinary commodity. It is indeed an addicting commodity and should not be treated in public or philosophical discourse or in law in the same manner as non-harmful, non-addicting commodities.[31] The same goes for other mood-altering, addicting drugs.

Key to minimising individual and social harms is the pragmatic dual approach of legal regulation and rigorous enforcement at societal levels. Comprehensive pragmatic solutions will inevitably need international support and agreement, especially as legal issues are tied up with a succession of international laws, the previously mentioned 'unchangeable' laws.

The whole debate on cannabis law — criminalisation, decriminalisation and regulation — has entered a new phase, especially as a result of changes in some US states[32], Uruguay[33] — in 2013 the first country in the world to legalise the sale, cultivation, and distribution of recreational cannabis — Canada[34] and developments in Europe. Austria, Malta, the Netherlands and Portugal, have already decriminalised the possession of small amounts of cannabis[35] as Germany too is processing drug reform legislation.[36]

The slow opening of gaps in prohibition will potentially cascade suggesting it might be better for governments to embrace not small, but large changes at an early stage to establish long-term a new regulatory system for distribution, sales and possession. Otherwise, bits of legislation will grow incrementally with one change added to deal with holes in previous efforts and in a manner that limits legislators' abilities to deal with legacy entitlements, inevitable commercial anomalies and the rising power of a new drugs industry. It would be better to embrace a comprehensive legislative change from the outset and for governments to lead and own it directly, and not leave it to market forces.

Alongside legislation, there is a need to address how existing criminal gangs can be disrupted and their members diverted, if possible, from their trade and from other criminality. Within a changed legislative environment, there should be an option to openly pursue and negotiate large scale amnesties for mid-ranking drug dealers who can demonstrate a capacity to cease their criminal activities. The tool of amnesty was used

The Harm Done

previously following the Good Friday Agreement to release prisoners who were sentenced for murder and other serious crimes during the Northern Ireland Troubles and can be used again to bring an end to drug wars. Alongside this, incentives for street runners, couriers, and day-to-day dealers should offer meaningful prospects of career or lifestyle changes. What difference would a change in policy make if the latter group — considered particularly marginalised — had no exit, no respite?

Unsurprisingly given my background, this book is an analysis of the drugs scenario, primarily as a problem — a three-faceted problem: personal, community and health / social. This is particularly the case for heroin. Of all illegal drugs it is considered to have most propensity to cause and prolong drug dependency, as well as contributing to and exacerbating other problems and harm. When I graduated from Trinity College in 1980 young people's heroin use was the predominant problem encountered by the social work service. It remained so, within a child welfare and protection perspective, for over two decades. Most people, I am sure, irrespective of their general attitudes to drug use and misuse, would be appalled and distressed to visualise a young person, or parent, injecting street-bought heroin with all the risks entailed in drug adulteration and contaminated injection equipment. Many might be further distressed, or at least surprised, to realise that by taking heroin the drug taker most likely experiences a high level of pleasure and euphoria and they might not be as feckless as they otherwise appear.

Less distressing perhaps is that codeine, the addictive across-the-counter pharmacy opiate, is relatively easily available. It is used for non-medical pleasure inducing purposes, potentially, by large numbers of drug takers. The level of its sales is unknown, as it does not require regulation. The drug is sold as a short-acting analgesic for mild to medium pain management. Those using it can experience pleasure and perhaps euphoria, depending on the quantities consumed. These codeine products are taken orally and the glass of water does not attract the attention that drug injecting does.

Using across-the-counter pharmacy codeine is not referenced as a health or social problem in the same manner as heroin. Concerns may be expressed about easy availability and the addiction problems caused for those who use codeine for a long time or as an enhancement with other drugs or alcohol.[37] It is speculated that some visitors to Ireland buy a codeine supply from pharmacies as it may not be so easily available back home. When purchasing codeine in pharmacies, there is a requirement that customers be routinely asked: 'Why do you need it?' The approach to this is lax with many chemists not operating the rule at all.[38] Nonetheless, having been tutored not to mention headaches or hangovers, many quietly murmur something about arthritic or back pain, while to themselves they think: 'Ahem! To help me get high, of course. Why else?'

Like it or not, getting high is a universally accepted form of celebration and of bringing pleasure into the everyday experience of life, work, family, sport and relationships. It can happen naturally through meditation, yoga, mindfulness, spirituality, or by reading, going to the cinema, theatre or exercise or spending time immersed in outdoor pursuits — hills, seas, forests. Getting high frequently happens with the assistance of alcohol, a practice deeply embedded in faith observance, celebrating sporting achievements, and in marking personal, family and community milestones, particularly in western societies and for sure in Ireland. Alcohol-fuelled weddings are regularly lampooned here on social media.

To repeat, alcohol carries a greater burden of disease in society than do illegal drugs. For the past five decades the World Health Organization has published several research reports and reviews that emphasise the causal connection between increased availability and accessibility of alcohol and ensuing problems of mortality and morbidity, including liver cirrhosis, traffic accidents and violence.[39] It contends that societies can, short of prohibition, reduce these problems primarily using measures to restrict and reduce alcohol consumption. These include increased taxation, licensing restrictions and drink-driving counter measures. A total ban on alcohol marketing is advocated. It is suggested that given the competing interests between the alcohol industry (shareholder profit) and government (population health) working in partnership would simply lead to 'ineffective policy'.[40]

In contrast to the public health approach, the drinks industry advocates the importance of individual change. Like other industries whose products cause harm, they tend towards sponsoring educational programmes that focus on individual decision-making and parental influences. Meanwhile, they avoid a consideration of the role played by advertising and corporate marketing as influencers in young people's choices. They do not reference at all the role played by taxation and marketing restrictions.[41] Drinkaware, funded by the alcohol industry, has provided training to secondary school teachers on how 'to lead classroom lessons about alcohol'.[42] The programme was described as 'bizarre' in 2019 by then Health Minister Simon Harris TD who added: 'It is not appropriate that schools use any materials or resources developed by organisations funded by the alcohol industry'.[43]

The Harm Done

At no time was the everyday normative use of alcohol more evident than in how it was discussed in the media and other public forums during the Covid-19 pandemic. Pressure mounted as Christmas 2020 approached for the reopening of pubs and bars, representing the long-awaited reopening of society. Unsurprisingly the move was followed by further restrictions arising from an increase in Covid-related deaths in January 2021.

At times major reopening announcements were accompanied on TV and radio by vox pops from people inside or outside pubs who eagerly awaited re-openings. Elsewhere, health managers struggled to have their voices heard on the likely negative impact of the change on over-stretched health care facilities. Reopening the economy and society seemed unhealthily preoccupied with the question posed by Tanaiste, Micheál Martin, TD: 'Where can we drink'.[44] A return to normality seemed reliant on opportunities for people — high on alcohol — to congregate in public places, dance in circles, hug and kiss with abandonment and explore relationship possibilities with new or random partners. There was little mention of the potential Covid-19-related harms to themselves or others.

Had the Covid-19 reopening debates included specialist cafes for cannabis or society clubs where members could safely consume cocaine or opiates, would the conversation have been more evenly balanced? Would it have been less dominated by the success or failure of a single industry built on consumption of one commodity? Any objective assessment of the relative social-distancing risks associated with imbibing alcohol rather than cannabis, for example, would have been, paradoxically more likely to conclude that the latter is less harmful.

If society dedicates so much time and resources to people getting high, then surely it should have a strong rationale for doing so and avoid the confusion caused by allowing one approach while outlawing others. It would be better to focus on how the options for getting inebriated can be best facilitated, harms best minimised, while stepping away from the 'drugs is a scourge' narrative. That latter idea makes sense only when the drug alcohol is included.

Three years after it was announced as an aim of Coalition Government (Fianna Fáil, Fine Gael, Green Party)[45] a motion to establish a Citizens' Assembly on Drugs Use was agreed by the Oireachtas in February 2023.[46] Two months previously an Oireachtas Justice Joint Committee recommended that Government pursue a policy of decriminalisation in 'respect of the possession of drugs for personal consumption'.[47] The recommendation reflected an emerging consensus among parliamentarians.[48] It was supported by political party leaders, Micheál Martin[49] and Ivana Bacik.[50]

The Citizens' Assembly on Drugs Use, 2023, was presented with mountains of evidence on different and contrasting strategies for dealing with drug issues in society. For virtually every well-researched proposal backing one policy idea, there are several other equally well-presented arguments against. It is reasonable to assume that the citizens deliberated on these arguments in a balanced manner.

Commencing its final gathering on October 21 2023, the assembly's first significant conclusion was an overwhelming vote to discontinue the current arrangements for managing drug problems through legal prohibition: a vote against the status quo. The Assembly then proceeded to recommend a comprehensive health-led approach for all drugs, within the existing, slightly tweaked, prohibition framework. The proposal is represented as a form of decriminalisation, whereby possession of drugs for personal use would continue to be illegal but would not be dealt with through the criminal code, but through health-led diversion. As possession remains illegal, the gardaí would continue to have rights of search and seizure, and in this regard, the recommendation falls short of 'decriminalisation'. Meanwhile the drug trade would remain in the hands of organised criminals.

A potential obstacle to Government proceeding with this approach is that in 2019 it already agreed to develop a health-led diversion scheme, but the legislation for this has yet to be processed. The scheme proposed brief-intervention alternatives to criminal prosecutions for the first two instances in which persons are found in possession of drugs for their own personal use. If ever introduced, it potentially offers more symbolic than real value. It can highly suggest that Government is adopting a more liberal approach. However, people who use drugs recreationally do not want or need a health intervention, although they may avail of it, as some do currently, in their efforts to avoid a custodial sentence through the courts. The client-centred basis of drug treatment indeed, is seriously undermined by such a scheme and would result in health care professionals being diverted away from more serious drug treatment as a result.

The current National Drug Strategy, 2017-25 furthermore, is already represented as a comprehensive health led approach. During assembly proceedings, there were several criticisms aired about the lack of progress in specific health-related measures, and it seems incredible that having voted against the status quo, assembly members proceeded to vote for continuing the same basic approach.

The Harm Done

The assembly's vote on the issue of cannabis 'legalisation / regulation' was particularly interesting. The voting method was proportional representation (PR) by single transferable vote. In the assembly, members voted for their preferred options, in separate ballots across a range of drug types, in order of choice. In this regard, 42% (36) of assembly members voted for 'legalisation / regulation' as the first of five options for dealing with cannabis, as compared to 27% (23) for the next highest option, which was 'comprehensive health-led approach'.

On the fourth count however, votes for the other three options had transferred to the 'comprehensive health-led approach' which went ahead of the 'legalisation / regulation' option by a single vote, 39 to 38. Thus, the legalisation option was defeated by a single vote in a PR system. This was quite extraordinary, especially as the legalisation option was quite specific as compared to the more qualified 'comprehensive health-led approach'. It begs the question why the assembly did not insist on putting a proposal yes / no for legalisation / regulation in the same manner it did with respect to continuing the status quo.

It was obvious from the proceedings that some assembly members were unhappy with the way the voting was conducted, especially as it was claimed by the assembly's chair that the voting was akin to general election voting. However, in elections people get to choose between definable entities, such as people or parties, whereas in the assembly the entities were variable and not easily compared. Following the vote, other votes provided for a detailed elaboration of the 'comprehensive health-led approach'. It identifies an array of service and funding proposals that are quite substantial. It is more of the same however and does not address matters in relation to stigma and marginalisation, which, as discussed in Chapter 9 are directly linked to the legal issue, and to the unwillingness of mainstream, non-specialist services to provide ongoing health and social care services to drug users.

It is important to note that citizens' assemblies can only make recommendations, and not policy decisions. Governments have found creative ways of ignoring recommendations in relation to drugs in the past and will willingly do so again. Given that 42% of assembly members, following a period of deliberation, voted in favour of legalisation, the omens are positive. This level of support can be built upon, especially through extending the debate into local communities, and into civil society, more broadly. The Citizen's Assembly on Drugs Use needs to be viewed simply as an important stage in the process of change: more deliberation, more debate are required.

The Harm Done

The War on Drugs has failed and along with it, prevention and treatment packages designed to mitigate the effects of prohibition, will fail also. Government must take responsibility and make a big decision, in much the same way that public health officials decided on the Methadone Protocol as stated at this chapter's outset. That said, a decision on a new way forward has to be taken openly and transparently.

Irish society is not secretive as it was forty-five years ago when heroin problems first manifested in poor communities and were later followed by AIDS. At the time, under new legislation, condoms could be bought but only through pharmacies on prescriptions issued for bona fide family planning purposes; divorce was prohibited; abortion was totally outlawed; sex between consenting males was legally disallowed; a tsunami of revelations of child sex abuse in families, institutions and elsewhere was yet to be unleashed; and meanwhile the first pope to step on Irish soil received a tumultuous whole-of-society welcome.

Times have moved on. People have over four decades of experience of the drug problem and the harm that was done either directly or to their parents and grandparents and in their communities and neighbourhoods. They have debated, protested and changed other things. They rowed in behind the Northern Ireland Peace Process despite misgivings on the peace credentials of key players. People can make mature, informed decisions about drugs and alcohol and they should be helped get on with it. Political leaders need to embrace the mantle of change. They need to make unchangeable laws, changeable.

A group of young people in Ballyfermot, early 1990s.
Photo: Derek Speirs ©

Planting an end-of-pandemic tree, Holly House, Ballybrack, December 2021
Photo: Barry Cullen

CHAPTER 11

Re-Imagining and Strengthening Community

This book opens in 1950s Ballyfermot when people were settling into the new public housing estate. At the outset, they came mainly from Dublin's inner city communities. Many of them were descended from nineteenth century rural migrants who, following famine and other disruptions, came to Dublin seeking work and refuge. They formed families and integrated into the city's sub-divided tenements and similar estates. Others came with the population movements of the post-Emergency (1940s and 1950s) as Ireland's transformation from rural to industrial society began to escalate. Our street, Ballyfermot Parade, had families from towns in Galway, Mayo, Roscommon, Wexford, Wicklow, and the Aran Islands to name but a few. In Ballyfermot, they joined their inner city Dublin counterparts as first came the houses, then the people and, away from the prejudices of external commentators and observers, they mixed, connected and found community.

During the 1950s, Dublin families accepted offers in inner city flat complexes such as St Teresa's Gardens where I worked (1980–85) Dolphin House, where I lived (1986–89) and Fatima Mansions. They were all built around the same time as Ballyfermot. But unlike it, the complexes were in the middle of familiar urban places and communities such as Dolphin's Barn, Rialto and the Tenters. In contrast to their monikers, they were four-storey flats, not houses, of good quality but hardly mansions and none had individual gardens.

By the 1970s several large public estates were completed on Dublin's outskirts, in Ballymun, Blanchardstown, Clondalkin, Coolock, Darndale and Tallaght. Eventually, arising from concerns that large public housing

The Harm Done

schemes inadvertently lead to a concentration of social problems, housing authorities stopped building these estates during the early-1990s, a position that has continued with successive governments. Is is now shown to have been fatal for contemporary housing supply, especially as it has been unable to replace it with an effective alternative for housing people who cannot afford to build or buy their own homes. Many people who grew up in large public housing estates however would stop short from advocating that more such estates be built if it meant that like previous house building these became marginalised estates. There is more to developing communities than simply building houses.

Mistakes were made in some of the house building projects. One perhaps was the failure to supply, in a timely manner, adequate infrastructure and facilities, particularly in suburban estates. As a result families felt isolated, forgotten. There was an inability to put into place effective estate management and maintenance facilities in complexes where dwellings were small, of high density and lacked clear boundaries between public and private spaces. Most importantly, however, was the institutional failure to present public housing positively. The underlying suggestion that 'homeowners made better citizens than renters'[1] prevailed reinforcing a negativity in tenants towards their own places. Potentially, those who saved and bought their own homes were perceived as better citizens inadvertently encouraging public housing tenants to view their estates negatively.

Yet, the original conception of these projects could not be faulted. Moreover, the state, without deference to either colonial legacy or religious governance, could point to them and proudly claim them as its own achievement. Public housing was one of the few genuine successes of the state's social policy, a policy that in other areas — health, education and social services — was assigned primarily to external, mainly religious bodies.

Today, when passing through Ballyfermot and other public estates, the presence of families from Eastern Europe or Africa, Asia, South America and the Middle East is visible and openly referenced. They seek new beginnings or are escaping social and economic stagnation, disruption, war and conflict, in much the same way as large numbers of Irish-born families have moved from land to city and beyond. Whether in the nineteenth century, the 1950s or more recently, families have sought income, employment and stability in the city, alongside accommodation in public and publicly funded housing, confirming,

Re-Imagining and Strengthening Community

were it needed, that migration and settlement are at the crux of urban history, and occasionally of urban conflict.

As a trained social worker I am conscious that community social work draws influence from the settlement movements of the late 1800s and early 1900s in Toynbee Hall (London), Hull House (Chicago), United Neighbourhood House (New York) and the work of the Civics Institute in Dublin. These bodies focused on supporting families settling into new places following migration or other disruptions. Places and communities thrive or stagnate on their ability to accommodate and support newcomers and their willingness to facilitate existing members to make open choices on local settlement or movement to new places.

Growing up in Ballyfermot, I never considered I was from a housing mistake or a deprived / disadvantaged area. I was never discomfited about my place. As a young adult I was conscious of labelling from others in their words or expressions especially after I answered the question: 'Where do you come from?' In taking a cue from my parents, I never accepted that the answer 'Ballyfermot' needed to be explained, but simply stated. In most instances, the response was fine, but I still recall my irritation with: 'And where are you from now?'; 'Haven't you done well for yourself?'; and worst of all from a geographically challenged Fine Gael acolyte in Trinity College in 1978: 'Ah yes, I thought you were from the northside alright.'

During its early decades, Ballyfermot was low income with limited social and physical infrastructure. For sure, there was no evidence of exceptional wealth. It certainly had its needs and included several residents who lacked essential means for a quality life. Many families needed external supports and services in dealing with everyday challenges. In my childhood, I knew of children who due to their social and family circumstances were always likely to have difficult lives and outcomes. Subsequently many did, especially in instances where family difficulties were compounded by the lack of income and an inability to find work, sometimes coupled with excessive alcohol intake, addiction and so forth. A few families were immersed in criminality and at times garnered more attention and notoriety, internally and externally, than their activities or numbers deserved.

Yet amid these adversities, most people showed tremendous resilience, were well grounded and later gave security and stability to their children, grandchildren and their wider families. Some furthermore have since provided guidance and leadership in community affairs, local government, trade unions, sports, arts, media, music and entertainment.

My serious involvement with community affairs commenced with a

The Harm Done

decision in 1975 to forgo employment offers in the civil service and private companies. Instead I took up a low-paid job at the Ballyfermot Playground. It was life-changing and I was indebted to playground leader Elizabeth (Mrs) Durham for encouraging me to choose this pathway. It exposed me to new thinking in community services, the role of women and the position of youth and children in society. By working in the playground and developing new community relationships, I built a connection with local people, children and young people and developed an interest in social sciences and community participation.

Studying social work in Trinity College taught me not only about psychosocial issues and interventions, but about collective advocacy and working with groups and communities. Practical placements helped expand my understanding of working people's lives and culture. I became aware of the importance of community work, of how in the background it could help bring about small, yet significant changes in everyday lives.

Although I never worked there again, my experience of Ballyfermot was always fundamental, setting a reference for whatever else I did, particularly from a work perspective. It discreetly guided me towards discovering contested notions of community. It helped me differentiate between grassroots models that brought people together to participate and develop leadership in resolving community problems, and other models that saw community as having relatively fixed structures, led by self-selected interests of religious, business, political and professional elites. Most importantly my Ballyfermot background helped me understand that collectively people can make change happen, albeit small, but change nonetheless.

During the early 1980s when a community model was advocated for drug treatment, I was one of only a few social workers assigned a community work role in local social work teams. In my case, this was in the south inner city. My main input was developing community leadership and exploring prevention and treatment responses. Similarly a colleague in north Dublin's Ballymun housing estate was considering responses to drug problems that included helping to establish the local Youth Action Project. Community workers in other areas were involved in leadership training although instead of drug issues they were mainly focused on community projects on women's health issues, Travellers' health and accommodation, and in developing family support services in new housing estates.

Over time social work personnel in these community work roles decreased, even as the overall number of social workers rose dramatically.

The fall reflected a general lack of interest by statutory bodies in employing community workers[2], A shift in state attitudes to the sector was evident when the Combat Poverty Agency was formed by statute in 1986. It had a specific remit to support community development in tackling poverty. Early on, it invested in pilot schemes for local women's groups, community art projects and local projects for tackling educational disadvantage. It generated research on community issues and produced papers and other relevant resource materials on topics such as community project management, evaluation and guidance for using the media, and policy development.[3] And it had an overall coordinating, support and advisory role with the Government's Community Development Programme (CDP) (1990–2009), the first to be funded exclusively with state resources.

Individual CDP projects had modest financial aid for staffing and operating costs. The programme started in 1990 with fifteen previously EU-funded projects (1985–89)[4] and quickly expanded to a hundred-and-eighty in total. The CDP asserted that community development could promote positive change in society by challenging the causes of poverty and offering opportunities to those lacking choice, power and resources. It advocated involving the poor in making changes they themselves identified as important and which drew from their own knowledge, skills and experience.

In the mid 1990s, due mainly to the growing number of community projects referencing drug problems in their work plans, the Combat Poverty Agency set up and funded a working group from CDP projects to develop drug policy issues and to organise a conference on their development.[5] At the same time these issues arose in the work of partnership companies set up under the Government's Local Development Programme (1994). For example, in 1997 the Canal Communities Partnership[6], reflecting the extent of drug issues in its first wave of community consultations, commissioned a feasibility study on a vocational rehabilitation service for problem drug users.[7] This led eventually to setting up the Turas training project which continues to operate.[8]

Community and local development programmes were central to considerations for forming local drug task forces following the Rabbitte Report (1996). Then Taoiseach John Bruton convened a meeting of the chairs of Dublin's partnership companies to explore ideas and proposals for setting these up.[9] Each company was asked to nominate a chairperson for task forces — all based in partnership areas — to help get them up and running. Later, the CDP had an important role in helping them to identify needs and assemble and train personnel to form and operate local drug projects and services. Thus community development played an early important role in establishing task forces and developing and implementing their work plans.

Less than two decades after the CDP was established, it was forced to wind down in 2009. The decision was controversial[10] and took place on the back of another a year earlier — to disband the Combat Poverty Agency.[11] Both decisions took place as recession began. It became clear Government was determined to impose expenditure cutbacks wherever it could withstand public pressure and to suppress, in so far as possible, independent critical voices.[12] An anti-society, anti-community narrative had gained traction in the run-up to the Celtic Tiger. This now found favour with a critical mass of Government ministers. It reached a reprehensible zenith during the recession and made way for a community development perspective more top-down than grassroots-informed.[13] And it put more emphasis on central planning than peoples' participation. Paradoxically, the failure to give coherent central direction and leadership to community projects contributed to their demise. Prior to the CDP's dismantling, individual projects had considerable autonomy, but little policy direction and some lacked coherent governance.

My involvement with the CDP at different stages was quite extensive, mainly through evaluation and consultancy support.[14] Through this involvement, it was always evident that when communities mobilised their shared human energies and resources to tackle deep-rooted social and economic problems, they could have a positive impact in ways not possible with an alternative process. This work was visible across a variety of domains: women, lone parents, rural development, co-operative enterprise, innovative training, alternative education, integrated service developments, and the mobilisation of people across housing, planning, unemployment, at-risk children, inter-generational poverty, ethnic and sexual identities, as well as drugs.

This work and more recently my work with DLR Drug and Alcohol Task Force, taught me there was something simple and practical about community development. It relied greatly on semi-structured conversations — one-to-one and in groups — to identify key players and potential leaders, doers with a record of concern about local problems. It helped identify people committed to further involvement and bringing in others: building rapport, and helping to develop insight into local conditions and experiences, generating ideas for new projects and services, for moving things on and thus changing people's circumstances.

Community work helps people to build connections and improve their ability to bring about change in their personal and social circumstances. It can help improve their health, living and social conditions and personal lives. It helps to create new social networks, restoring people's belief in the value of place. It generates hope in the potential of working together to reframe social issues and to advocate for public services that are more accessible and adaptable to local and community needs.

In my view the paid community worker has a critical role in supporting the process, but the role is preferably background, out of the limelight, helping community leaders to emerge and supporting them in developing and maintaining foreground positions. This latter dimension helps people to transform their situation in the long term. It is often compared to the facilitative role exercised in casework. As in most areas of professional work, the skills required for community workers arise from intensive training, and on-the-job mentoring, supervision and support. They do not just happen. As in any field, people doing the same job over a long period with poor supports and supervision can lose their way and become ineffective in their roles. No community worker indeed, is as ineffective as the one who believes they have been uniquely picked to fulfil the role, and who proceed to do so without management support and guidance.

While I fully support the importance of training local community workers, I do not agree with the proposition that because a person is local or of a marginal group / community or identity, they are best or solely equipped to be a community worker or to articulate community needs. Nor do I agree with the suggestion that people who are recovering from addiction or who share lived experiences make the best drug workers or that those with a record of mental health issues make the most effective therapists.

Usually, background life experiences bring unique insights into, and informed perspectives on, the issues being tackled. On their own they can lack more general impact. In my experience, whatever a person's background, which for obvious reasons is not always shared or known by others, factors such as empathy, a willingness to learn and be taught non-directive and facilitative skills, good training and continuous support and supervision, and an ability to see the bigger picture — these are what create the most effective community / drug workers and, indeed, social workers.

Despite a continuous lack of funding for community bodies and services, many people spend a sizeable portion of their life journeys developing resourceful neighbourhood connections, organising together in advocacy groups or developing accessible, needs-based services. In the space of a few weeks after the Covid-19 emergency was declared in March 2020, thousands of community organisations up and down Ireland mobilised to support a joint collective response. While most institutions closed, several community personnel arranged for outdoor facilities to ensure ongoing contact and engagement with vulnerable groups such as the elderly, young people at risk and families struggling to make child care arrangements.

For a short period, the pandemic transformed society. The state moved centre stage, replacing the private market as the fulcrum for housing, incomes, community and social supports. Health care, normally a mix of public and private services and long seen to reinforce inequalities, was briefly almost nationalised. An improved coordination of services to vulnerable drug users was impressively implemented. Several homeless individuals and families at direct risk of Covid-19 infection were successfully accommodated during 2020–21.

Irish society's response to the virus showed that well-organised and accountable community structures matter, that individual private interests are, whether we like it or not, linked to the common interest. The anti-society narrative of the late 1970s — just as the opiate epidemic in Dublin took root — reached its pinnacle at the outset of the 2008 recession. But it does not reflect people's desire for a genuine, non-individualised social contract. They want and deserve better. Almost fifty years after the first pilot programme on community development — funded through European sources — it is time to move away from pilot community schemes. Community development needs to be more reliably funded, with proper structures for developing and supporting the work.

This work deserves better state and institutional support in providing the necessary funding and employment and proper supervision of community workers and care personnel to promote and develop autonomous community groups and bodies. These should have appropriate structures and be free from political and other interference. They have a particularly important role to play in responding to, preventing and treating drug problems, especially where these are experienced in patterns associated with other localised social issues.

Trained community workers can play an important role in helping communities to promote the common interest, to help identify those who are most vulnerable and marginalised, helping them confront pressing issues, and tackle social problems, including drug problems. They can also help people overcome harm, personal trauma and conflict.

Universities and other learning and training bodies can play a role in mentoring and qualification opportunities, making the preparation and training of community workers more mainstream in social / youth work, continuing education and other disciplines. With adequate supports, community can take on creative innovative meanings, with greater attention to local services than those at higher levels. Community has its limitations and can too often be concerned with narrow self-interests or with unreal ambitions around political mobilisation. With a strong focus on social solidarity, human rights and community participation, particularly at times of recurring or immediate crisis, it can support better public health and housing, more equality and help to reduce and mitigate drugs and other societal problems. By rebuilding communities and strengthening neighbourhood connections with substantial investment in community services, and reclaiming community development, society can reduce some of its deepest social problems, including with drugs.[15]

In the 1980s and 1990s it was local services and community bodies, and not the health services, that initiated and led debates on the nature of society's response to drug problems and the need for targeted, localised actions from preventative and treatment perspectives. Their grassroots missions contributed greatly to developing harm reduction, methadone maintenance and the formulation of national strategies. Irrespective of the outcomes from other processes, it will take a consolidated demand from a wide range of bodies to develop and achieve a new united platform on drug policy reform. Community bodies, other grassroots movements and local services need to be part of that process. In the wake of cutbacks and a serious disrupting of the sector in recent years, however, it would need renewed leadership structures and organisational resources for a debate such as this to be adequately facilitated.

In the midst of a confused and at times contradictory societal response to emerging issues — for example current inward migration and refugee issues arising from the war in Ukraine — Government has acknowledged the absence of mechanisms to consult communities. It had one fifteen years ago and dismantled it with its own decisions. Successive administrations have not fixed this. It is obviously too late for Government to rebuild these mechanisms from the ground-up so that a coherent community voice could be articulated now. But there is scope for it to do so. It is time to get on with it and in doing so institute a coherent, policy-driven structure at national level to develop, support and resource community development.

Notes and References

Introduction Endnotes

1. Mayo, M. (2017). 'The slippery concept of "community" both locally and transnationally' in M. Mayo, *Stories of Migration, Displacement and Social Cohesion*. Bristol: University Press / Policy Press.
2. Freyne, P. (2023). 'Refugees welcome: "Chanting get them out to the most vulnerable. What does that achieve?"' *Irish Times,* Jan 28.
3. Conlon, C. (2022). 'Nimbys need to realise their objections to new housing harms all of society', *Irish Examiner*, Dec 26.
4. McTeirnan, A. (1993). 'Drug needle plan runs into trouble', *Irish Times*, May 11.
5. Kelleher, P., Whelan, M. (1992). *Dublin Communities in Action*. Dublin: Combat Poverty Agency / Community Action Network.
6. Power, C., O'Connor, R., McCarthy, O. and Ward, M. (2012). 'Credit unions and community in Ireland: Towards optimising the principle of social responsibility'. *International Journal of Co-Operative Management*, 6 (1), pp. 10–22.
7. Bolger, P. (1977). *The Irish Co-operative Movement: Its History and Development*. Dublin: Institute of Public Administration.
8. Motherway, B. (2006). *The Role of Community Development in Tackling Poverty in Ireland*. Dublin: Combat Poverty Agency.
9. Government of Ireland (2019). *Sustainable, Inclusive and Empowered Communities: A five-year strategy to support the community and voluntary sector in Ireland, 2019–2024*. Dublin: Department of Rural and Community Development.
10. Pobal (2020). *Community Services Annual Report 2019*. Dublin: Department of Rural and Community Development.
11. O'Gorman (2020). *Community Drug Projects: Responding to drug-related harms from a community development perspective*. Dublin: Citywide.
12. Kelleher, P., O'Neill, K. (2018). *The systematic destruction of the community development, anti-poverty and equality movement (2002–2015)*. Cork: Kelleher Associates.
13. Over the last four decades different terms have been used, in policy and practice, in reference to people who use drugs. During the 1980s they were referred to by most services as 'drug abusers' or 'heroin abusers'. For a while in the 1990s it became 'substance misusers', and during the HIV / AIDS crisis there were references to 'intravenous drug users' (IVDUs) and then 'problem drug users' (PDUs). More

recently the terminology 'persons who use drugs' (PWUDs) seems to apply. I have concluded that whatever the language, and I particularly dislike abbreviations when applied to people, that for as long as drugs are prohibited, people who use them will be stigmatised. In this book I have kept the term 'drug user', and occasionally interchanged this with 'drug taker' and sometimes also I differentiate 'recreational drug user' and 'problem drug user'. In general I find the term 'drug user' least cumbersome from a reading / writing perspective.

14 National Coordinating Committee on Drug Abuse (1986). *First Annual Report,* Dublin: Author. In addition to a selection of public servants the committee included three external drug 'experts' from the non-governmental sector, each of whom were openly dedicated to the 'War on Drugs' rhetoric. In addition, the report's contents were decidedly pro-abstinence, anti-methadone and anti-liberalisation.

15 An official move toward a new approach commenced with the *Government Strategy to Prevent Substance Misuse, 1991* which, for the first time, referenced 'harm reduction' as an aim of policy and also established two pilot community drug teams.

Chapter 1 Endnotes

1 Dunne, S. (1966). 'Adjournment Debate — Ballyfermot (Dublin) Amenities'. *Dáil Debates.* Thursday, 10 February, Vol. 220 No. 9.
2 O'Sullivan, R. (1999). '"Sensational Reporting" blamed for negative image of public housing'. *Irish Times,* October 29.
3 RTÉ Archives (1971). 'Life in Ballyfermot'.
4 Larkin, K. (2006). 'Traveller Community' in K. Larkin *Ballyfermot: Building a Community, 1948–2006).* Dublin: Author, pp45.
5 Jackson, V. (1996). Letter to the Editor — Semperit Closure, *Irish Times.* Dublin. Sept 26.
6 Leonard, S. (2021). 'Point in Time: Ballyfermot's lost jewel'. *Tallaght Echo.*, October 7.
7 https://dublintenementexperience.wordpress.com/2014/02/25/a-shared-tenement-story-from-jim-meade/
8 Dublin City Council (2017). *The History of Social Housing in Inchicore.* Dublin.
9 McCaughren, T. (1973). 'Rent according to means', *RTÉ Archives.*
10 Fogarty, M. (1942). *Planning and the Community.* Oxford: Catholic Social Guild.
11 Come Here to Me (2015). 'A Spectre is Haunting Ballyfermot: The 1952 Co-Op Scandal'. *blog.*

Chapter 2 Endnotes

1 Wormell, D. (1984). Interview with Trevor Danker, *Sunday Independent,* cited in F. Douglas (1984). *The History of the Irish Pre-school Playgroups Association,* Dublin: Irish Pre-School Playgroups Association, published online, 2018, by OMEP Ireland, p34. Download (Jun 17, 2023) at: https://omepireland.ie/wp-content/uploads/2019/07/History-of-the-IPPA.pdf

Notes and References

2. McGee –V– The Attorney General and Revenue Commissioners (1974). *Supreme Court of Ireland Decisions.*
3. Shatter, A. (1978). 'How the Supreme Court has Muddled the Censorship Issue' *Magill*, Sept 1.
4. National Committee on Pilot Schemes to Combat Poverty, 1974–1980 (1980). *Final Report.* Dublin: Department of Social Welfare.
5. RTÉ Archives (1976). 'Machinery Replaces Men.'
6. RTÉ Archives (1971). 'Life in Ballyfermot'.
7. National Committee on Pilot Schemes to Combat Poverty, 1974–1980 (1980). Op Cit.
8. 'Who Speaks For Us?' (1979). *Liberty People*, No. 3, Jul.
9. 'A Tuppence Halfpenny Committee' in *Strumpet*, Vol. 1, No. 2 (Mar), 1981.
10. Skehill, C. (1999). *The Nature of Social Work in Ireland: A Historical Perspective.* New York: Edwin Mellen.
11. Ibid.
12. Fahey, T. (2007). 'The Catholic Church and Social Policy' in Healy, S., Reynolds, B. (eds.).*Values, Catholic Social Thought and Public Policy,* Dublin: Social Justice Ireland.
13. Harrison, P. (2021). *Hanged If You Do. Reflections from a career in child protection.* Dublin: Open.
14. Ó'Corráin, D. (2022). 'The Catholic Church, the State and Society in Independent Ireland, 1922–2022' *Working Notes.* Dublin: Jesuit Centre for Faith and Justice, Jan 21.
15. Freire, P. (1970) (1993).*Pedagogy of the Oppressed.* London: Penguin (Random House).
16. Kelleher & Whelan, (1992). Op. Cit.
17. Rothman, J., Erlich, J., Tropman, J. (eds.) (2008). *Strategies of Community Intervention.* (7th edition). Peosta, IA: Eddie Bowers Publishing Company.
18. Brager, G., Specht, H. (1973). *Community Organising.* New York City: Columbia University Press.
19. Mayo, M. (1975). 'Community development a radical alternative?' in Bailey, R., Brake, M. *Radical Social Work.* London: Edward Arnold. Available as download.
20. *National Committee on Pilot Schemes to Combat Poverty, 1974–1980 (1980).* Op. Cit.
21. Casey, M. (1992). *What are we at? Ministry and Priesthood for the Third Millennium.* Dublin: Columba Press.
22. Smith, M. (1997, 2002). 'Paulo Freire and informal education', *The encyclopaedia of pedagogy and informal education.* Download (Jul 2, 2023).at https://infed.org/paulo-freire-dialogue-praxis-and-education/
23. Earley, C. (ed) (1992).*Parish Alive Alive Oh! Ten Dublin parishes the story and challenge.* Dublin: Columba Press, p43.
24. Kelleher and Whelan, (1992). Op. Cit.

Chapter 3 Endnotes

1. For an overview of Community Care Programme see National Economic and Social Council (NESC). (1987). *Community Care Services: An Overview, Report No.84,* Dublin: Author.

The Harm Done

2. Skehill, C. Op. Cit.
3. The memorandum is cited in Working Group on Community Development Policy in the Eastern Health Board (1994). *Discussion Document on Community Development Within the Eastern Health Board,* Dublin.
4. Community News (1979). 'Rubbish Riots in Teresa's Gardens' *Liberty People,* No. 3, Jul.
5. Rudd, J. (1979). *Out In The Cold — A Report on Unattached Youth in Dublin in the Winter of 1978/79,* Dublin: HOPE
6. Anonymous (1981). 'Harvest of Misery' *Strumpet — Dublin City News Magazine,* Vol 1(1). Jan pp 28–32. Although this article is referenced as anonymous it was penned by Frank Deasy (1959–2009), a co-founder of the Ballymun Youth Action Project.
7. Lally, C. (2020). 'Larry Dunne: The life and death of a notorious Dublin drug dealer', *Irish Times,* May 19.
8. Hartnoll, R. (1986). *Drug use in Europe,* Druglink, Sept/Oct, p15 Download (Jun 20, 2023). at https://www.drugwise.org.uk/wp-content/uploads/SeptOct8613.pdf
9. Law, B. (1972). *Developments in the Irish Drug Scene,* National Drug Advisory and Treatment centre (unpublished).
10. Harty, T. (1975). 'Services for Drug Users' in *Contacts, Journal of the Eastern Health Board,* vol. 1, no. 2.
11. Butler, S. (1991). 'Drug problems and drug policies in Ireland: A quarter of a century reviewed.' *Administration,* 39 (3), 210–233.
12. *Report of the Working Party on Drug Abuse,* (1971). Dublin: Stationery Office.
13. https://www.irishstatutebook.ie/eli/1977/act/12/enacted/en/html
14. Parker, H., Bury, C., Eggington, R. (1998). *New Heroin Outbreaks Amongst Young People in England and Wales,* Police Research Group, Paper 92. London: Home Office.
15. Advisory Council on the Misuse of Drugs (ACMD). (1998). *Drug Misuse and the Environment,* London: Stationery Office.
16. O'Donoghue, N., Richardson S. (1984). *Pure Murder — A book about drug use.* Dublin: Womens Community Press, p25.
17. Walsh, C. (1984). 'Centre for Drug Addicts Opened', *Irish Times,* Oct 28.
18. Preble, E., Casey, J. (1969). 'Taking Care of Business: The heroin-user's life on the street'. *International Journal of Addictions,* vol 4 (1), p2.
19. Anonymous (1981). Op. Cit.
20. Cullen, B. (1983). *Fighting Back.* Dublin: St Teresa's Gardens Development Committee. Download (Apr 25, 2023). at https://www.drugsandalcohol.ie/5517/
21. Kelly, M. (1982). *Submission to Task Force on Drug Abuse.* Dublin: Eastern Health Board.
22. O'Kelly, F., Bury, G., Cullen, B., Dean, G. (1988). 'The rise and fall of heroin use in an inner city area of Dublin', *Irish Journal of Medical Science,* Vol 157 (2), p35–38.
23. National Coordinating Committee on Drug Abuse (1986). *First Annual Report.* Dublin: Author.
24. *Minutes of a Special Meeting of the Dublin City Council held in the Council Chambers, City Hall, Cork Hill, on Tuesday 13th Oct at 6.45pm.*

Notes and References

25 Dean, G., Bradshaw, J., Lavelle, P. (1983). Drug Misuse in Ireland, 1982–1983; Investigation in a North Central Dublin area and in Galway, Sligo and Cork. Dublin: Medico-Social Research Board, p3.

Chapter 4 Endnotes

1. Kearney, N. (1982). 'How do services meet the needs of the poor?' in *Conference on Poverty 1981: Papers at the Kilkenny Conference, 6th–8th Nov 1981.* Blackrock, Dublin: The Council for Social Welfare (A committee of the Catholics Bishops' Conference).
2. Musto, D. (1999). *The American Disease: Origins of Narcotic Control* (3rd ed), Oxford University Press.
3. Blackman, S. J., Bradley, R., Fagg, M. and Hickmott, N. (2017). 'Towards "sensible" drug information: critically exploring drug intersectionalities, "Just Say No," normalisation and harm reduction'. *Drugs: Education, Prevention and Policy.* 25 (4), 320–328.
4. McGrath (2016). 'Nancy Reagan and the negative impact of the "Just Say No" anti-drug campaign' *The Guardian*, Mar 8.
5. https://www.europa.eu/system/files/media/publications/documents/779/TDXD14015ENN_final_467020.pdf
6. Yates, R. (2011). "Therapeutic Communities: Can-Do Attitudes for Must-Have Recovery', *Journal of Groups in Addiction & Recovery,* 6:101–116.
7. https://www.philadelphia-association.com/
8. O'Hagan, S. (2002). 'Kingsley Hall: RD Laing's experiment in anti-psychiatry', *The Guardian*, Sept 2.
9. Hornik, R., Jacobsohn, L., Orwin, R., Piesse, A. (2008). 'Effects of the National Youth Anti-Drug Media Campaign on Youths'. *American Journal of Public Health,* 98(12).
10. Lilienfeld, S., Arkowitz, Hal. (2013). 'Just Say No?' *Scientific American Mind,* 25(1).
11. Ashton, M. (1999). 'The danger of warnings', *Drug and Alcohol Findings,* 1, p22.
12. McBride, S. (2000). 'You should perhaps consider going round to schools and advising youngsters of the terrible effects of drugs,' Judge McBride tells defendant. *Irish Independent.* May 12.
13. https://lionsclubs.ie
14. 'Lions launch "War on Drugs"', (1983). *Irish Times,* Feb 1.
15. Humphreys, K., Wing, S., McCarty, D., Chappel, J., Gallant, L., Haberle, B. (2004). Self-help organizations for alcohol and drug problems: Toward evidence-based practice and policy, *Journal of Substance Abuse Treatment,* 26, 151–8.
16. Emrick, C. D., Tonigan, J. S., Montgomery, H. and Little, L. (1993). Alcoholics Anonymous: What is currently known?, In *Research on Alcoholics Anonymous: Opportunities and Alternatives* (Eds, McCrady, B. S. and Miller, W. R.). Rutgers Center of Alcohol Studies, New Brunswick, NJ.
17. https://www.alcoholicsanonymous.ie/new-to-aa/the-twelve-steps/
18. The Minnesota Model's leading exponents in Ireland include Aiséirí, Hope House and the Rutland Centre.

The Harm Done

19 Butler, S., Jordan, T. (2007). 'Alcoholics Anonymous in Ireland: AA's first European experience', *Addiction,* 102.
20 In the early nineties the NDATC was relocated to a purpose-built facility in Trinity Court, Pearse Street, with a change of title to Drug Treatment Centre Board.
21 The level of first admissions into county-based Irish psychiatric hospitals and units for alcohol disorders peaked in 1982 at 2,518, or 26% of all first admissions, and 103.3 per 100,000 of the population (The Report of a Study Group on the Development of Psychiatric Services [1984] *The Psychiatric Services — Planning for the Future.* Dublin: Stationery Office). The report, advocated that these problems should be dealt with in community settings. The planned reduction in alcohol admissions was initially slow and in 2006 it was advocated that addiction be de-coupled completely from psychiatric services save in instances of co-related psychiatric disorders (Department of Health and Children [2006] *Report of the Expert Group on Mental Health Policy: A Vision for Change.* Dublin: Stationery Office). Over the period, 1998–2018, the level of first admissions for alcohol fell from 43.8 to 8.2 per 100,000 population (Millar, S. (2020). 'Trends in alcohol and drug admissions to psychiatric facilities' *Drugnet Ireland,* Issue 74, Summer 2020, p28–29.).
22 Raftery, M. (1982): 'Heroin: The Sweet Dream of Death', in *In Dublin,* May 13 (p22). Rafferty quotes extensively from a NDATC spokesperson.
23 O'Donoghue & Richardson, (1984). Op. Cit.
24 Comberton, P. (undated). 'Peggy's Story', *50 Faces* —28 — *Coolmine TC,* Download (Jul 24, 2023). at https://www.coolmine.ie/50-faces-28/
25 This information was in a quarterly journal published by Daytop in 1981. 'Sam Anglin along with his wife, Maggie, were dispatched to Dublin in February 1981 to assume the Clinical Directorship of Coolmine and the dividends surfaced swiftly. A Coolmine graduate, Thomas McGarry, came to Daytop for training and under Sam's guidance will blossom before long into the Director's spot at Coolmine'. Cullen, B. (1991). *Community and Drugs – a case study in community conflict in the inner city of Dublin.* MLitt thesis, Trinity College Dublin (submitted as Kieran Cullen). p20.
26 Anglin, S. (1982). 'Coolmine director: Interview', *Irish Press,* Feb 3. Re-check
27 Comberton, J. (1983). 'Letter to Lord Mayor, Ald Alexis Fitzgerald', Oct 12. *Minutes of a Special Meeting of the Dublin City Council held in the Council Chambers, City Hall, Cork Hill, on Tuesday 13th Oct at 6.45pm.*
28 A pamphlet from Coolmine explains this approach as follows: "The primary psychological goal is to change the person's negative patterns of behaviour, thinking and feeling that predispose drug use; the main social goal is to develop a drug free lifestyle ... healthy behavioural alternatives to drug use are reinforced by commitment to the rejection of drugs, the creation of an anti-drug culture, to viewing drug-use as a cop-out" (Coolmine Lodge Therapeutic Community,1983, cited in B. Cullen, (1991). Op. Cit.).
29 Ahlstrom, D. (1987). 'Government's programme on disease spread defended', *Irish Times,* Sep 8. Cites James Comberton, at the fourth European Conference on Therapeutic Communities, which was hosted by Coolmine and addressed by

Comberton, Coolmine's Executive Chairman and President of European Federation of Therapeutic Communities.
30 Comberton, J. (1983). *Drugs and Young People*. Dublin: Ward River Press, cited by C. O'Donovan, Review, in *The Furrow*, 34(9), 597–599.
31 Kelly (1982). Op. Cit.
32 Brecher EM (1972). *Licit and Illicit Drugs, Consumers' Union Report*. Boston: Little Brown.
33 See *Coolmine Annual Report (2020)*. Download (Apr 30, 2023). at https://www.drugsandalcohol.ie/34580/
34 O'Donoghue & Richardson (1984). Op. Cit.
35 De Leon, G., Unterrainer, H. (2020). 'The Therapeutic Community: A Unique Social Psychological Approach to the Treatment of Addictions and Related Disorders' *Frontline Psychiatry*, 11.

Chapter 5 Endnotes

1 *Evening Press*, Apr 30, 1982; *Irish Times*, Apr 30, 1982 and *In Dublin*, May, 1982.
2 Rogers, H.(1981). Feature article in *Evening Herald*, Aug 30.
3 O'Kelly, et al (1988). Op. Cit.
4 Rafferty, M. (2012). (Opinion). 'Gregory deal would have had huge impact if fulfilled', *Irish Times*, Mar 9.
5 14 Years for Larry Dunne (1985). *RTÉ Archives*, May 23.
6 STGDC (1984). Speech by committee's chairman, Paul Humphrey to a seminar on drug problems, organised by the Labour Party in the Gresham Hotel Dublin, Feb 5.
7 Cullen, B. (1991). *Community and Drugs – a case study in community conflict in the inner city of Dublin*. MLitt thesis, Trinity College Dublin (submitted as Kieran Cullen). p86.

Chapter 6 Endnotes

1 See, for example: News Collection (1985). 'St Teresas Gardens' *RTÉ Archives*. In addition to this news item on RTÉ, the *Today Tonight* programme also had a filmed report and studio coverage.
2 Drink and Drug News — DDN (2014). 'London Calling'. *DDN Newsletter*, Download (Jun 18, 2023). at: https://www.drinkanddrugsnews.com/london-calling/
3 This project was established as Baptist church ministry and had both a caring and pragmatic approach to drug problems: 'There is no simple and immediate way of preventing some people from trying to destroy themselves, but in the longer term it is possible to improve the social experience of a group so that they become more interested in fulfilling themselves than in destroying themselves. It is necessary that a community gives all its members hope for a reasonably happy life. Communities of all kinds can be dynamic or apathetic, just or unjust, kind or cruel, exciting or dull. Whenever individuals or groups in a community are dropping out and being self-destructive, the community needs to be involved in the process of rehabilitation' (Blakeborough, E. [1977]: A *Community Response to Drug Abuse*. Kingston upon Thames:

The Harm Done

      Kaleidoscope Youth and Community Project). The project remains in existence at https://kaleidoscope68.org/kaleidoscopes-story/

4. Over 45 years after it was established Lifeline collapsed as an independent charity in 2017 amidst allegations of poor financial control systems (Brindle, D. [2017] 'Drug and alcohol charity Lifeline Project collapses' *The Guardian*, May 18.

5. SCODA was a national coordinating group for UK voluntary bodies involved with drug issues. It provided a forum for exchanging information and ideas and for promoting research. It was established in 1972 and in 2000 it merged with the drug information and library body, the Institute for the Study of Drug Dependence (ISDD). to form Drugscope (2000–2015). ISDD was established in late 1968 and produced the highly regarded periodical, *Druglink*, now archived at https://www.drugwise.org.uk/druglink-archive/

6. Strang J., Gossop M. (eds). (1994). *Heroin Addiction and Drug Policy: The British System*. Oxford: Oxford University Press.

7. Edwards, G.(1969). 'The British approach to the treatment of heroin addiction' *Lancet*, 293(7598), p768–772.

8. Brecher (1972). Op. Cit.

9. See for example the controversy over the downgrading of Navan Hospital. Walsh, L. (2021). 'Navan hospital-downgrade protest draws up to 10,000 people' *Irish Times*, Oct 30.

10. Butler, S. (2016). 'Coolmine Therapeutic Community, Dublin: a 40-year history of Ireland's first voluntary drug treatment service.' *Addiction*, Vol 111 (2).

11. Desmond, B. (1983). *Dáil Debates*, Dec 6.

12. Ibid.

13. Niland (1983). Op. Cit.

14. O'Mahony, P., Gilmore, T. (1982). Drug Abusers in the Dublin committal prisons, cited in Butler, S. (2015). 'Coolmine Therapeutic Community, Dublin: a 40-year history of Ireland's first voluntary drug treatment service' *Addiction*, Sept.

15. Fennell, N. (1984). 'Misuse of Drugs Bill (Second Stage)' *Debates*, Tuesday Jun 19. Vol. 351 (8).

16. Brecher EM (1972). *Licit and Illicit Drugs, Consumers' Union Report*. Boston: Little Brown.

Chapter 7 Endnotes

1. 'Labour Youth condemns attack' (1984). *Irish Times*, Feb 23.

2. Desmond, B. (1983). 'Questions — Oral Answers: Ministerial Task Force on Drug Abuse'. *Dáil Éireann debate*, 6 Dec Vol. 346 No. 6.

3. Ibid.

4. Niland, G. (1983). 'Tough love for drug kids', *Irish Times*, Jun 16.

5. In Dec 1984, the Minister for Health, Barry Desmond TD, announced he was considering favourably any submission the National Federation of Community Action on Drugs made with respect to funding services in addition to that already being provided with government support in Dún Laoghaire, his constituency. See *Dáil*

Notes and References

Éireann debate –Thursday, 13 Dec 1984, Vol. 354 No. 12.
6   Farrell, M. (1983). 'The armalite and the ballot box', *Magill*, Jun 30. Downloaded (Jun 12, 2023). at https://magill.ie/archive/armalite-and-ballot-box
7   In 1997, Caoimhghín Ó Caoláin, became the first Provisional Sinn Féin candidate to be elected to the Dáil, and to take up a seat. Currently (2023), Sinn Féin has 36 sitting TDs, out of a total of 160.
8   Heaney, M. (2012). 'The battle for political supremacy in the newsroom', *Irish Times*, Jan 3.
9   Yeates, P. (1984). 'Shooting linked to drive on pushers' *Irish Times*, Mar 22.
10 Ibid.
11 Yeates, P. (1984). 'Was "The General" the target of IRA Group?' *Irish Times*, March 24.
12 News (1984). 'Four men convicted of Crumlin Kidnap and Garda shooting' *Irish Times*, Jul 26.
13 Brophy, E. (1984). 'People who took on the pushers' *Sunday Press*, Feb 26, 1984.
14 Editorial (1984). *Irish Times*, Mar 1. The editorial described the march as 'one of the most persuasive seen in a long time' and that it 'deserves to succeed' and that the marchers 'have a right to resent being branded as vigilantes'.
15 Bennett, D. (1988). 'Are They Always Right?' in *Whose Law and Order—aspects of crime and social control in Irish Society*, edited by M. Tomlinson, T. Varley and C. McCullagh. Dublin: Sociological Association of Ireland.
16 Cullen B. (1991). *Community and Drugs – a case study in community conflict in the inner city of Dublin*. MLitt thesis, Trinity College Dublin. p89 (footnote).
17 Yeates, P. (1984). '150 protest at arrest of drugs campaigners' *Irish Times*, Mar 29.
18 NicMhurchadha, A. (1984). 'Sinn Féin and Drugs', Letter, *Irish Times*, May 18.
19 '"Free State" not a target — IRA' (1984). *Irish Times*, Jan 6.
20 Ó Faoleán, G. (2023). 'Armed robberies, kidnappings and counterfeit cash: The many ways the IRA sought to finance itself during the Troubles' *Irish Times*, Mar 11.
21 Murtagh, P. (1983). 'Soldier and garda killed as Tidey is freed', *Irish Times*, Dec 17.
22 Moloney, E. (1983). 'Gunmen were doing their duty — Adams', *Irish Times*, Dec 19.
23 Ireland (1998). 'Family of murdered garda finds IRA releases too high a price to pay for peace', *Irish Times*, May 23.
24 Report (1990). 'Court told of gun battle as six jailed over bank raid' *Irish Times*, Jul 3.
25 Muire Tynan, M. (1995). '12 more IRA prisoners for release today under scheme' *Irish Times* Jul 29.

Chapter 8 Endnotes

1   Cullen, B. (1989). *Community Organisations and the Media: A guidebook to using the media for community and voluntary organisations in Ireland*. Dublin: Combat Poverty Agency.
2   Cullen, B. (1989). *Poverty, Community and Development: A report on the issues of social policy that have arisen in the work of the nine projects of the Second European Programme to Combat Poverty, 1985–1989*. Research Report Series no. 4. Dublin: Combat Poverty Agency.

3   Cullen, B. (1988). 'Heroin at the heart of the Irish AIDS problem', *Irish Times,* Jan 28.
4   'AIDS scare prompts policy re-think in Scotland' (1988). *Druglink*, Nov/December, p5. Download (Jun 20, 2023). at https://www.drugwise.org.uk/wp-content/uploads/NovDec8614.pdf
5   Newcombe, R. (1987). 'High time for harm reduction', *Druglink*, January / Feb, pp9–10.
6   Advisory Council on the Misuse of Drugs (ACMD) (1988). *AIDS and Drug Misuse: Part One*. London: The Stationery Office.
7   Cassin, S. (1991). 'Drug users and AIDS' *Irish Times*, letter to the editor, Nov 11.
8   Gusfield, J. R. (1996). *Contested meanings: the construction of alcohol problems*, University of Wisconsin Press, Madison, Wisconsin.
9   Advisory Council on the Misuse of Drugs (ACMD) (1982). *Treatment and Rehabilitation*. London: The Stationery Office.
10 Edwards, G. and Gross, M. M, (1976). Alcohol dependence: Provisional description of a clinical syndrome, *British Medical Journal*, 1(6017), 1058–61.
11 European Monitoring Centre for Drugs and Drug Addiction (EMCDDA). (2016). *Perspectives on Drugs: The role of psychosocial interventions in drug treatment*. Lisbon: Author.
12 Miller, W. R. and Weisner, C. M. (2002). *Changing substance abuse through health and social systems*. New York / London: Kluwer Academic / Plenum.
13 Murphy, I. (1990). 'HIV and Drug Treatment — Issues and Policies', *AIDS Inform*. pp 8–10.
14 DeLargy, I. (2018). *20 Years of the Methadone Treatment Protocol*. Dublin: Irish College of General Practitioners.
15 Scully, M., Pomeroy, L., Johnson, Z., Johnson, H., Barry, A. (1991). 'Observed patterns of HIV related risk behaviour amongst intravenous drug users attending a Dublin needle exchange in its first year (AIDS Resource Centre, 19 Haddington Road, Dublin)' in N. Lorimer, R. Schmid and A. Springer, *Drug Addiction and AIDS*. New York: Springer-Verlag.
16 Ibid.
17 Murphy, I. (1990). 'HIV and Drug Treatment — Issues and Policies', Dublin: *AIDS Inform*, p8–10.
18 Cullen, B. (1992). 'Director's Report' *Ana Liffey Drug Project Annual Report, 1991*. Dublin: Ana Liffey Drug Project, pp10.
19 Schmidt, W. (1993). 'To Battle AIDS, Scots Offer Oral Drugs to Addicts' *The New York Times,* Feb 8.
20 O'Mahony, T. (1990). 'Drug treatment policies and the challenge of HIV' *AIDS Inform*, Vol 2(3), p4–5.
21 Ana Liffey Drug Project. (1990): *Drug Treatment Policies — A discussion document*. Dublin: Author.
22 Ana Liffey Drug Project. (1990): *Annual Report 1990*. Dublin: Author. p10.
23 Cullen, B. (1994). 'Community drug treatment: an untried response to drug problems in Dublin'. *Irish Social Worker,* 12, (2), pp. 16–18.
24 News Briefs (1990). 'Drug Workers' Forum' in *AIDS Inform*, Vol 2 (2).

Notes and References

25 Ana Liffey Drug Project. (1990): *Annual Report 1990*. Dublin: Author. p18.
26 Ibid.
27 Ibid, p9.
28 National Coordinating Committee on Drug Abuse (1991). *Government Strategy to Prevent Drug Misuse*. Dublin: Author.
29 Murphy, I. (1990) 'The Irish College of General Practitioners Policy Statement on Illicit Drug Use and Problems of Drug Addiction (Oct)— A Review', *AIDS Inform*, Vol 2(3), p6.
30 *First Report National Coordinating Committee on Drug Abuse* (1986). Dublin: National Coordinating Committee on Drug Abuse, p9.
31 Butler, S. (2002).'The making of the methadone protocol: The Irish system?' *Drugs Education, Prevention and Policy*, 9 (4).p311–324.
32 McTeirnan, A. (1993).'Drug needle plan runs into trouble', *Irish Times*, May 11.
33 Maher, J. (1995).'EHB to open drug clinic despite picketing', *Irish Times*, Oct 18.
34 O'Halloran, M. (1999).'Anger in Tallaght over addict centre', *Irish Times*, Jul 8.
35 News Briefs (1990).'Community Response' in *AIDS Inform*, Vol 2 (3), p2.
36 Dublin City Council (1991).'Reception of deputation from Community Response', *Minutes of a Quarterly Meeting of the Dublin City Council, held in the Council Chamber, City Hall, Cork Hill, on Monday, 8th Apr, 1991, at 6.45 pm*. Dublin: Author.
37 Community Response (1991).*A report of a seminar on drug problems in the south inner city held in Kevin Street College of Technology on Nov 3rd, 1990*. Dublin: Author.
38 https://communityresponse.ie/
39 McCabe (1997).'Citywide Drugs Crisis Campaign', in Healy, G. (2000). *Drugs Poverty and Community Development: A report of the Conference for Community Development Programme Projects on Community responses to Drugs Issues, held in Feb, 1997*, Dublin: Combat Poverty Agency.
40 https://www.citywide.ie/what-we-do/
41 Bowden, M. (1997).*Community Addiction Response Programme CARP Killinarden: review and interim evaluation report, final revised draft*. Dublin: Community Addiction Response Programme.
42 https://tallaghtdatf.ie/community-projects/
43 https://rialtocommunitydrugteam.org
44 Bowden, M. (1996).*Rialto Community Drug Team: policy discussion paper*. Dublin: Rialto Community Drug Team.
45 Ibid.
46 Ministerial Task Force on Measures to Reduce the Demand for Drugs. (1996). *First report of the Ministerial Task Force on Measures to Reduce the Demand for Drugs*. Dublin: Stationery Office.
47 There is a broad categorisation of *supply reduction* and *demand reduction* in drug strategies across different jurisdictions. Ireland's current *National Drug Strategy, 2017–25*, has itemised five separate goals, two of which (1) and (2) correspond to demand reduction (prevention, harm reduction and treatment), goal (3) corresponds to supply reduction, while goals (4) and (5) refer to the participation and evidence mechanisms

that are in place to support and delivery on other elements.
48. First Report to Government from Co-ordinating Group of Secretaries (1994), cited in Murray, J. (2001). *Reflections on the SMI* (Strategic Management Initiative), working paper, Policy Institute, Trinity College. Accessed, Sep 24, https://wwwha.tcd.ie/policy-institute/assets/pdf/PIWP01_John%20Murray.pdf
49. Department of Tourism, Sport and Recreation (2001). *National Drug Strategy: Building on Experience, 2001–2008.* Dublin: Stationery Office, p126.
50. *National Drugs Strategy (Interim), 2009–2016* (2009). Dublin: Department of Community, Rural and Gaeltacht Affairs.
51. Department of Health (2017). *National Drug Strategy, Reducing Harm Supporting Recovery, 2017–25.* Dublin: Author.

Chapter 9 Endnotes

1. Bennett, J. (2006). *Vital connections. Local Drug Task Forces — Leading the response. Conference report.* Dublin: Local Drug Task Force, Chairs & Coordinators Network.
2. Gossop, M., Marsden, J., Stewart, D., Kidd, T. (2003). The National Treatment Outcome Research Study (NTORS): 4–5 year – follow-up results, *Addiction*, vol 98(3), 291–303.
3. Ward, J. (1997). *Methadone Maintenance Treatment and other Opioid Replacement Therapies*, London: Taylor & Francis.
4. Comiskey, C., Kelly, P., Leckey, Y., McCulloch, L., O'Duill, B., Stapleton, R., White, E. (2009). *The ROSIE Study: Drug treatment outcomes in Ireland,* Dublin: National Advisory Committee on Drugs.
5. Ministerial Task Force on Measures to Reduce the Demand for Drugs. (1996). Op. Cit.
6. Smyth, B., O'Brien, M. (2004). 'Children attending addiction treatment service in Dublin, 1990–1999. *European Addiction Research*, 10, pp. 68–74.
7. https://www.hse.ie/eng/services/list/5/addiction/yoda/
8. Department of Health and Children. (2005). *Report of the working group on treatment of under 18 year olds presenting to treatment services with serious drug problems.* Dublin: Stationery Office.
9. Smyth, B. (2022). 'Sanctions for the Possession of Certain Amounts of Drugs for Personal Use: Discussion. *Oireachtais debates, Joint Committee on Justice.* Tuesday Jul 12.
10. www.dlrdatf.ie
11. DLR — Community Addiction Team https://dlrcat.ie/
12. Dún Laoghaire Rathdown Outreach Project http://www.drop.ie/
13. https://dlrcat.ie/services/family-support.html
14. https://dlrdatf.ie/site/assets/files/1061/barnardos_fis.pdf
15. (1). https://dlrcat.ie/services/youth-programme.html (2) https://www.myp.ie/services-for-youths/ (3) http://www.southsidepartnership.ie/Old/index.php/loughlinstown
16. See: (1) Hidden Harms https://dlrdatf.ie/site/assets/files/1061/barnardos_fis.pdf (2) Youth-at-risk network, https://dlrdatf.ie/site/assets/files/1055/youth_at_risk_brochure_jun_15.pdf, and (3) Integrated Collaborative Practice Programme, Prendiville, P. (2016) *Integrated Collaborative Practice Programme — Evaluation Report*, Dublin: Southside

Notes and References

Partnership (Training), Dún Laoghaire Rathdown Drug and Alcohol Task Force, Community Action Network (CAN), Department of Adult and Community Education, Maynooth University.

17 See list of local and regional task forces on the following website https://dlrdatf.ie/about/
18 *National Drugs Strategy (Interim), 2009–2016* (2009). Dublin: Department of Community, Rural and Gaeltacht Affairs.
19 *Statista Q*, Download (Mar 7, 2023) at https://www.statista.com/statistics/433207/current-healthcare-expenditure-ireland/
20 National Drugs Strategy 2001–2008: *Rehabilitation. Report of the working group on drugs rehabilitation*. Dublin: Department of Community, Rural and Gaeltacht Affairs.
21 Durkan, B. (2021). *Oireachtas Debates: Joint Committee on Health debate* — Wednesday, 1 Dec.
22 Shorthall, R. (2022).*Oireachtas Debates: Joint Committee on Health debate: National Drug Strategy*. Wednesday, 19 Jan.
23 Crowe, C. (2022). *Oireachtas Debates: Joint Committee on Health debate: National Drug Strategy*. Wednesday, 19 Jan.
24 Healy, R. (2021). *Nothing about us without us: the current voices of the Irish methadone service users. [Draft]*. Dublin: Service Users Rights in Action (SURIA).
25 Johnston, L., Liddell, D., Browne, K., Privadarshi, S. (2017). *Responding to the needs of ageing drug users: Background paper commissioned by the EMCDDA for Health and social responses to drug problems: a European guide*. Lisbon: European Monitoring Centre for Drugs and Drug Addiction.
26 Mayock, P., Butler, S., Hoey, D. (2018). *'Just Maintaining the Status Quo'? The experiences of Long-Term Participants in Methadone Maintenance Treatment*. Dublin: Dún Laoghaire Rathdown Drug and Alcohol Task force (in conjunction with Community Addiction Team, Sandyford, and Southside Partnership).
27 Mayock, P., Butler, S. (2021). 'Pathways to 'recovery' and social reintegration: The experiences of long-term clients of methadone maintenance treatment in an Irish drug treatment setting' *International Journal of Drug Policy*, 90, Apr.
28 Mayock, P. Butler, S. (2022): '"I'm always hiding and ducking and diving": the stigma of growing older on methadone', *Drugs: Education, Prevention and Policy, 29(2)*.
29 https://www.canaction.ie/our-work-human-rights-service-users-rights-in-action/#:~:text=SURIA,on long-term methadone treatment.
30 National Drug Rehabilitation Implementation Committee (2010). *National Rehabilitation Framework Document*, Dublin: Health Service Executive.
31 Ibid.
32 Bryan, A., Moran, R., Farrell, E., O'Brien, M. (2000). *Drug-Related Knowledge, Attitudes and Beliefs*. Dublin: Health Research Board.
33 Dillon, L.(2017). 'General public attitude to drug users – CityWide survey' *Drugnet Ireland*, 61, Spring, p. 7.
34 A 2021 review of of 22 studies of supervised drug injecting facilities found that reductions in opioid overdose morbidity and mortality, improvements in injecting

behaviours and improvements in access to treatment facilities were among the outcomes reported. There was no impact on crime or public nuisance. (Levengood, T., Yoon, G., Davoust, M., Ogden, s., Marshall, B., Cahill, S., Bazzi, A. (2021) 'Supervised Injection Facilities as Harm Reduction: A Systematic Review' *American Journal of Preventive Medicine*, 61 (5), 738–749.).

35 European Monitoring Centre for Drugs and Drug Addiction (EMCDDA) (2022) *Spotlight on Drug Consumption Rooms (website update)*. Lisbon: Author. https://www.emcdda.europa.eu/spotlights/drug-consumption-rooms_en

36 Department of Health (2017) *National Drug Strategy, Reducing Harm Supporting Recovery, 2017–23*. Dublin: Author.

37 https://www.gov.ie/en/publication/39e48-national-oversight-committee/#terms-of-reference-for-the-noc-2021-2025

38 The National Drug Strategy has been based in different government departments since the publication of the Rabbitte Report in 1996. As an interim, and while arrangements were being put into place to develop the strategy overall, responsibility lay with the Office of An Taoiseach. It then moved to the Department of Tourism, Sport and Recreation, which published the 2001–2008 National Drug Strategy. The Department of Community, Rural and Gaeltacht Affairs published the 2009–2016 Strategy while the Department of Health published the 2017–25 Strategy.

39 Kirby, J. (2023) Case Study: Integrated Service Delivery in Cork and Kerry, input by Joe Kirby, HSE Social Inclusion Manager into Citizen's Assembly on Drugs Use, Jun 24.

40 Clondalkin Drug and Alcohol Task Force (2018). *Clondalkin Drug and Alcohol Task Force strategic plan 2018–2025. Reclaiming community development as an effective response to drug harms, policy harms, poverty and inequality*. Dublin: Clondalkin Drug and Alcohol Task Force.

41 Department of Health (1980). *Task Force on Child Care Services: final report to the Minister for Health*. Dublin: Author.

42 European Monitoring Centre for Drugs and Drug Addiction (2016). *Perspectives on drugs: the role of psychosocial interventions in drug treatment*. Lisbon: Author.

Chapter 10 Endnotes

1 Bennett, J. (2006). *Vital connections. Local Drug Task Forces — Leading the response. Conference report*. Dublin: Local Drug Task Force, Chairs & Coordinators Network.

2 Over the period 2001–2006, international and domestic speakers at the Addiction Research Centre (ARC) conferences included: Michael Agar, (1947–2017), Judith Aldridge, Thomas Babor, Joe Barry, Ivana Bacik, Philip Bean, Philippe Bourgois, Shane Butler, Julian Cohen, Gemma Cox, Barry Cullen, Mary Cullen, Elliott Currie, Eilis Gilvarry, Ide Delargy, Margaret Hamilton, Harold Holder, Ann Hope, Eamon Keenan, Harald Klingemann, Karol Kumpfer, Fergus McCabe (1949–2020), Paula Mayock, David Moore, Tim Murphy, Ian O'Donnell, Howard Parker, Stanton Peele, Eoin Ryan, Betsy Thom, Jeff Ward, and Marguerite Woods.

3 Cullen, B. (1998). (Ed.). *Young People and Drugs: Proceedings of a half-day seminar held Nov*

Notes and References

22, 1997 at *Trinity College Dublin*. Dublin: Children's Research Centre, Trinity College Dublin.
4   Cullen, B. (1998a). 'Young Irish drug users and their communities' in B. Cullen (1998). Op. Cit.
5   Parker, H., Aldridge, J., Measham, F. (1998). *Illegal Leisure: The Normalization of Adolescent Recreational Drug Use*. London: Routledg.
6   Parker, H. (1998). 'The process of normalisation of recreational drug use amongst young people in the UK' in B. Cullen (1998). Op. Cit.
7   Murphy, T. (1996). *Rethinking the War on Drugs in Ireland*. Cork: Cork University Press.
8   Murphy, T. (2002). 'Drugs and Crime — Response Paper Summary' in *Debating Public Policies on Drugs and Alcohol, Second Annual Conference*. Dublin: TCD Addiction Research Centre. Download (Mar 10, 2023). https://www.drugsandalcohol.ie/3691/1/1767-1692_Debating_Public_Policies_on_Drugs_Alcohol.pdf
9   Mongan, D., Millar, S., Galvin, B. (2021) *2019/20 Irish National Drug and Alcohol Survey*, Dublin: Health Research Board, p80.
10 McCreery, S. Keane, M. Bowden, M.(2021). *Debts, threats, distress and hope: towards understanding drug-related intimidation in Dublin's North East Inner City*. Dublin: Ana Liffey Drug Project, p62.
11 Gallagher, C. (2023). 'How drug debts are used to control Irish communities: "Men are forced to go to jail on someone's behalf"' *Irish Times*, Apr 1.
12 Youth Workers Against Prohibition' (2021). *Change Starts with You*. Dublin: Author.
13 Freyne, P. (2021). 'Irish youth workers have banded together to seek an end to drug prohibition to remove criminal risk from users' *Irish Times*, Jul 3.
14 Joint Committee on Arts, Sport, Tourism, Community, Rural and Gaeltacht Affairs (2006). *The Inclusion of Alcohol in a National Substance Misuse Strategy*. Dublin: Houses of the Oireachtas.
15 Ibid, p9.
16 Nutt, D. (2010). 'Drug harms in the UK: a multicriteria decision analysis'. *Lancet*, Nov 6;376(9752):1558-65.
17 Millar, S. (2019). Cannabis use in Ireland. New findings from the fourth general population survey. *Drugnet Ireland*, Issue 68, Winter 2019, pp. 18–19.
18 GBD 2016 Alcohol Collaborators. (2018). 'Alcohol use and burden for 195 countries and territories, 1990–2016: a systematic analysis for the Global Burden of Disease Study 2016'. *The Lancet*, 392, (10152), pp. 1015–1035.
19 GBD 2016 Alcohol Collaborators. (2018). 'The global burden of disease attributable to alcohol and drug use in 195 countries and territories, 1990–2016: a systematic analysis for the Global Burden of Disease Study 2016', *The Lancet (Psychiatry)*, 12, 987–1012.
20 Kabir, Z., Gilheany, S., McKinney, E., Kit, K. (2022). *Global Burden of Disease: Estimates of alcohol use and attributable burden in Ireland. What the data tell us and what we need to do to address the burden of alcohol*. Dublin: Alcohol Action Ireland and UCC School of Public health.
21 All EU member-states are signatories to the United Nations Single Convention on Narcotic Drugs (1961, 1972). In addition all are affected by Council of the European

Union (2004). Council Framework Decision 2004/757/JHA of Oct 25, 2004.
22 Mc Dowell, M. (2006). (Minister for Justice). *Dáil Éireann debate* — Wednesday, 24 May, Vol 620, No. 2
23 Dillon, L. (2022). 'The cannabis policy debate', Drugnet, Issue 82, pp5–7.
24 Mc Dowell, M (2023). 'My view is that' *Seanad Éireann debate,* Thursday, 23 Feb, Vol 292, No. 5.
25 Leaders (2022). 'Joe Biden is too timid. It is time to legalise cocaine — The costs of prohibition outweigh the benefits' *Economist,* Oct 12.
26 Royal Society for Public Health (2016). *Taking a new line on drugs.* London: Author.
27 O'Riordáin, (2023). 'Fundamental reform of drug policy needed' *Press statement* coinciding with Labour Party submission to Citizens' Assembly on Drug use.
28 Government of Ireland (2022). 'Minister McEntee to reform Ireland's antiquated licensing laws' *Press Release,* Oct 25.
29 Kent, D. (2023). 'Advertising watchdog to review rules on zero-alcohol products' *Irish Examiner,* Jun 28.
30 McCambridge, J., Mialon, M., Hawkins, B. (2018). 'Alcohol industry involvement in policymaking: a systematic review', *Addiction,* 113, 1571–1584.
31 Ibid.
32 Leeds Matthews, A., Hickey, C. (2023). 'More US states are regulating marijuana. See where it's legal across the country' *CNN News,* Apr 27.
33 Goni, G. (2017). 'Uruguay, the first country where you can smoke marijuana wherever you like' *The Guardian,* May 27.
34 Government of Canada (2018). *Cannabis Legalization and Regulation.* Ottawa: Author.
35 Boffey, D. (2021). 'Malta to legalise cannabis for personal use in European first', *The Guardian,* Nov 13.
36 Under new German government proposals, adults (over 21 years) will be permitted to purchase up to 50g a month from a licensed non-profit club with maximum 500 members; young people aged 18–21 will be allowed 30g per month. Individuals will also be allowed grow up to three plants at home for personal use. Other proposed regulations relate to locations of clubs, opening times and restrictions around use of cannabis in public places. See: Scally, D. (2023). 'Germany scales back cannabis law reform' *Irish Times,* Apr 12.
37 McMurrow, C. (2022). '"It was 90 tablets a day" — Recovering codeine addict' *RTÉ News.* Oct 5.
38 McMurrow, C. (2022). 'Over-the-counter codeine rules to be reviewed — Health Minister' RTÉ News, Oct 14.
39 Babor, T., Casseell, S., Graham, K., Huckle, T., Livingston, M. Osterberg, E., Rehm, J., Room, R., Rossow, I. (2023). (3rd edition). *Alcohol: No Ordinary Commodity,* Oxford: Oxford University Press.
40 Babor, T., Casseell, S., Graham, K., Livingston, M. Osterberg, E., Rehm, J., Room, R., Rossow, I. Sornpausam, B. (2022). (3rd edition). 'Alcohol: No Ordinary Commodity — a summary of the third edition' *Addiction,* 117 (12) 3024–3036.
41 van Schalkwyk, M., Petticrew, M., Nason, M., Hawkins, B. (2022). 'What do we know

Notes and References

42. Casey, J. (2022). 'Alcohol body offering teachers training about drinking despite health department advice', *Irish Examiner,* Oct, 2.
43. O'Brien, C. (2019). 'Harris criticises drinks industry role in educating schoolchildren about alcohol', *Irish Times*, Nov. 27.
44. Martin, M. (2023). Comment about alcohol in *Talking Bollox Podcast*, episode 120. Apple Podcasts.
45. *Programme for Government — Our Shared Future* (2020).
46. 'Citizen's Assembly on Drugs Use: Motion', *Dáil Éireann debate* -Tuesday, 21 Feb 2023 Vol 1033 (6).
47. Joint Committee on Justice (2022). *Report on an Examination of the Present Approach to Sanctions for Possession of Certain Amounts of Drugs for Personal Use*. Dublin: Houses of the Oireachtas.
48. Ibid.
49. Martin, M. (2023). Comment about decriminalisation in *Talking Bollox Podcast*, episode 120. Apple Podcasts.
50. Loughlin, E. (2023). 'Labour leader Ivana Bacik backs licensed sale of cannabis at festivals', *Irish Examiner*, Mar 25.

about the alcohol industry's engagement with youth alcohol education?' *Blog*, Institute of Alcohol Studies, London School of Hygiene and Tropical Medicine.

Chapter 11 Endnotes

1. McHugh, E. (2023). 'I Like Public Housing and So Should You' *Blog*, Communities and Tenants Union (CATU).
2. Skehill, (1999). Op. Cit.
3. Combat Poverty Agency (2000) *The role of community development in tackling poverty*. Dublin: Author.
4. Cullen, B. (1994). *A Programme in the Making*. Dublin: Combat Poverty Agency. see Google Books link at https://www.kfcullen.ie/previously-published-report.html
5. Healy, (2000). Op. Cit.
6. The Canal Communities Partnership was established under the Government's Local Development Programme in 1994 and covered the areas of Bluebell, Inchicore, Kilmainham and Rialto. It later amalgamated with other partnership bodies as Dublin South City Partnership. https://dublinsouthcitypartnership.ie
7. McKeown, K. (1998). *Feasibility study on a drug rehabilitation service in Canal Communities*. Dublin: Canal Communities Partnership.
8. https://www.turastraining.ie/
9. At the time I was interim chairperson of the Canal Communities Partnership and attended this meeting on the partnership's behalf.
10. O'Regan, D. (2010). 'Communities "reeling" at closure of community projects', *Magill*, Feb 4. Download (Mar 7, 2023). at https://magill.ie/society/communities-%E2%80%98reeling%E2%80%99-closure-community-projects
11. Opinion (2008). 'The Combat Poverty Agency has been a stone in the shoe of successive

governments because of its work in raising public awareness' *Irish Times*, Aug 23.
12 Kelleher, P., O'Neill, K. (2018). *The systematic destruction of the community development, anti-poverty and equality movement (2002–2015)*. Cork: Kelleher Associates.
13 Harvey, B. (2015). 'Local and Community Development in Ireland' in C. Forde, *et al.*, *The Changing Landscape of Local and Community Development in Ireland: Policy and Practice Forde*. Cork: Institute for Social Sciences in the 21st Century University College.
14 This involvement included providing consultancy support to the programme overall, in 1988–89, 1992–95 and 2007–8, as well as a more direct research involvement with individual projects in Mounttown, Priorswood and Rialto, and also producing a video, *Making Inroads* for CAN in 1994/1995 — with inputs from community projects in Ballymun, Blanchardstown, Connemara (Galway), north inner city, Kilrush (Clare), Loughlinstown, Mayfield (Cork) and Wexford, and other videos for CAN in 2012 about its models of leadership training.
15 O'Gorman, A., Driscoll, A., Moore, K., Roantree, D. (2016). *Outcomes: Drug harms, policy harms, poverty and inequality*. Dublin: Clondalkin Drug and Alcohol Task Force.

Acknowledgements

At an early stage in writing this book, Professor Mary P. Corcoran (Maynooth University) and Professor William Molloy (University College Cork) were encouraging and generous with their time and feedback. The book has been transformed considerably since, but I appreciate that at this early stage they both took time out to immerse themselves in the text and to provide challenging feedback, most of which I have drawn from in developing later drafts.

My siblings Brian, Don, Denis, Owen and Eilish, and my niece Sian, commented on chapters about Ballyfermot, helping me to relive and reflect on that experience, as did Ken Larkin from the Ballyfermot and St Marks Heritage Group.

My undergraduate, mentor, and friend, Mary Whelan (1941–2022) and her partner Michael Casey, read through an early draft and provided constructive and enthusiastic feedback.

Separate meetings with Dr Matt Bowden Technological University Dublin), Dessie Martin (1960–2023), John Moylan and Rev Seán McArdle helped to clarify information about St Teresa's Gardens during the 1980s. Also exchanges with Patricia Daly and Terrie Kearney helped me fill some of the gaps in information about health board contacts. Ongoing discussions with Mary Doheny and Alan Hendrick helped trigger my memory about other relevant events during that period, and both have always been supportive of the project.

Michael Lacey — EHB and Community Response — Ray McGrath, Dr Marguerite Woods — both formerly of Ana Liffey Drug Project — helped me recall the work of the project during the early 1990s. Tony McCarthaigh from Rialto Community Drug Team also helped in verifying some details about the drug team and the early stages of drug task forces.

My colleagues from Dun Laoghaire Rathdown — Sandra Campbell, Mary Daly, Natalie Donegan, John Doyle, Ger FitzPatrick, Marie Kavanagh, Sandra King, Vivienne McCann and Kevin Webster — were

The Harm Done

particularly supportive and provided information about contemporary developments.

My friend June Meehan was a strong supporter from the outset and read three different versions and made detailed comments. She engaged with me in several intense discussions around the project's purpose, structure and direction. Her questions and reflections were always challenging, and she steered me with sensitivity towards a final structure. My friends Tony Byrne, Joe Duffy, Úna Lernihan, Mary McStay, Liam Maguire, Frank Murtagh and Noelle Spring, both collectively and individually, provided strong encouragement in the book's completion.

Thelma Blehein, Eddie D'Arcy, Jack Dunphy, Dave Little, Anthea McTiernan and Erna O'Connor also made comments for which I am grateful.

My nephew, Dr Niall Cullen (University of the Basque Country), undertook a copy-edit during 2022, and made important comments about structure and style, while Therese Caherty did a comprehensive pre-publication proof-read. Chenile Keogh carefully managed the project through its final stages.

The photographs are from Clodagh Boyd, Don Cullen, Paul Humphrey Collection, Aindriú Ó Conaill, Tony O'Shea, and Derek Speirs. The cover photo is also from Derek. The photo of Nancy Reagan visiting Daytop was provided by Alamy.

Dr Shane Butler (Emeritus Fellow Trinity College Dublin), who wrote the foreword, read the book, at different stages, three times, and his input was critical in identifying the material I should keep or set aside.

On several occasions my partner, Pat Tobin, helped me talk through different drafts, reminding me, as she often does anyway, that I 'already made that point.' Along with our adult children, Leeroy and Chelsea, she has given unflagging support and encouragement.

Finally, I have dedicated the book to Paul Humphrey (1959–2009), and I wish to acknowledge the contribution he made to community work in the 1980s. He was an unsung hero in the field: always there, but behind the scenes; supportive without interfering; present but never dominant. At a personal level, he left an enduring legacy, particularly for those who knew and loved him.